THE HAMMERS

Zan Swartzberg

Author: Zan Swartzberg

Complied and edited by: Lorraine Barbara Houston

Published by Lorraine B. Beigley

ISBN :9 780995 519534

Dedicated to:

The men and women who volunteered; giving of their skills

For some, they gave the ultimate gift – their lives.

Introduction

During the years 1947 – 1949 some eight hundred young South African Jews made their way by sea, land and air to Palestine to help the fledgling State of Israel fight the might of seven Arab countries.

These men and women, some of whom were veterans of World War Two, knew that they faced impossible odds when statistics showed they were joining 350,000 Jews who would battle against 300 Million Arabs.

A shuttle service from South Africa to Israel was founded by Pan African Air Charter, transporting young volunteers. Our South African Government were aware of these volunteers who were heading off to fight for a foreign land and turned a blind eye. We will always be thankful for that.

From these 800 young South African volunteers a cohort of around 120 formed the core of the fledgling Air Force, which included fighter pilots, bomber pilots, air gunners, navigators, bombardiers, radio operators and meteorologists. The remaining volunteers were integrated into the other areas of the armed forces, such as; tank brigade, artillery, medical, navy, aeronautical and mechanical division. All were selected as specialists in their respective fields of expertise.

They joined a further 2700 volunteers from 37 countries and became known as the 'Mahal'

The story that follows is about my own involvement in this battle and comprises of my own views and experiences.

Zan.

How it all began: Recruitment.

Early in 1947 whilst working at Rand Radio in Johannesburg, Mendy Vons and I joined a long queue at the Zionist Federation after hearing, on the grapevine, that they were recruiting volunteers for the Israeli Forces. I had an interview there with Phil Zuckerman who wanted to know my qualifications. I told him that I was a Ham Radio Operator, and had studied, by correspondence, with the National Schools in California, specialising in radio and electronics.

Phil suggested that I study and do the necessary examinations to obtain an International Radio Operator's licence. He arranged for me to enrol and study at the local Technical College. Within a few months I wrote and passed the required test. However, before I could obtain the full licence it was necessary to complete some flying time with a commercial airline, and this was arranged for me with Pan African Air Charter.

About this time the Federation bought some old British built Avro Anson twin engine aircraft, which had seen better days. These had been used all over the world to train bomber pilots and navigators. I believe that, in their newer days, they were used as operational bombers.

Mendy and I were delegated by the Zionist Federation to evaluate one of the aircraft and ready it to fly to Israel. The aircraft was parked at the Wonderboom aerodrome, north of Pretoria, which at that time was just bare 'veld' with a control tower mounted on crooked wooden poles. It has since been built into a very modern airport with the most up to date navigational systems. However, at the time, it suited our purposes, situated in the back of beyond with all the privacy that we needed.

When we arrived, we met Tittlestad, an ex-RAF pilot who was to take us up on a half hour test flight. We inspected the aircraft, noting that it was an early 1930 aircraft with tears in the fabric. The aircraft had a valid airworthiness certificate from the Civil Aviation Authority, so we took off on our test flight. It was a terrifying experience for me. The wind blew through the fuselage holes like a tornado and the noise and vibration was awful. As this was my first flight it probably felt worse than it was. We duly reported back to Zuckerman the defects we had found, including that the radio equipment did not work.

The Federation duly arranged for mechanics to go out to the airfield and work on the aircraft. They put at our disposal a Plymouth motor car and, at the crack of dawn each day, we would leave Johannesburg to drive to Pretoria. We spent each day doing our renovations and test flying the aircraft. Neither of us had a motor car drivers' licence, but we felt very important with the given responsibility. I was just nineteen and Mendy was twenty-two years old. Mendy had served as a radio operator with the South African Air Force and had earned his 'half wings' during the 1939-1945 conflict.

We patched up, to the best of our ability, the tears in the fabric with the result that we finally achieved a state of repair that would allow us to fly the aircraft to its desired destination.

We then started to plan our navigational route up Africa. We decided that the range of the fuel tanks, which were standard equipment in the aircraft, would not suffice for the long hauls between out stops. The planned route was Pretoria to Bulawayo, Salisbury, Ndola, Kampala, Entebbe and then further north towards Khartoum and then to our most northerly stop of Wadi

Halfa where we would turn east to Haifa via the Red Sea and the Gulf of Aquaba, all of which meant flying over huge areas of inhospitable desert.

Without permissions and contrary to all Civil Aviation regulations, we decided to extend the range of the fuel tanks. This we did by purchasing two forty-four-gallon drums from one the local oil companies. We installed these in a tandem fashion linked by rubber tubing. The drums were mounted on the floor in the centre of the fuselage and joined into the existing system with rubber tubing. Stop cocks were installed at strategic positions to the main tanks so that we could switch over when needed.

With this work completed it was decided that the weight of the fuel tanks added to the weight of a three-man crew would make the flight dangerous so Tittlestad and Mendy were to fly the plane to Israel and I would undertake my first trip on Pan African Air Charter to complete my radio operators licence.

We arranged with one of the oil companies to deliver our fuel and the tanker duly arrived with 'avgas (aviation gasoline) to top up our tanks. What the driver thought of our internal tanks, I wouldn't like to speculate! Once fuelled and all checks done, they duly took off due north into the wild blue yonder. Had they only known what the future held for them!

Pan African Air Charter

PAAC, as we fondly abbreviated Pan African Air Charter, was founded and funded by some very far sighted gentlemen in the Zionist Federation. The main reason, I believe, was as a shuttle service for volunteers to Israel, and bringing them home. Private passengers were accommodated in a small way, paying for their flights, especially when we did the European run. The postal service was also a very important link with Israel in those days. Considering that Israel was under a state of siege, and on a war footing, I don't think that any other commercial airline had a service running to that part of the Middle East.

The founders did not endear themselves at times, as they would suddenly arrive in the most unexpected places and decide to come along for the ride. The result was that if we had a full complement of passengers, two were summarily advised to wait for the next flight. As the majority of passengers were young Mahalnicks, or volunteers, eager to get to Eretz (Israel) and fight Arabs, you can imagine their disappointment. In some cases, they may have to wait a month for the next flight. Since our passengers were non-paying, they did not have much choice.

In the 1940's and 1950's the international airport in Johannesburg was Palmeitfontein. This was our main base of operation and from there we would head north. Our manifest was usually made out for a flight to Italy, but on leaving African shores we would quietly divert to Haifa over the Red Sea. Coming in to Haifa we would line up our approach to the runway with the Haifa Refining oil storage tanks.

In Haifa we had permanent rooms booked at the Central Hotel, and our contact was a very likeable chap by the name of Hans Weisbrod. A real mensch[i].

Another charter company, Westair, owned by PAAC but run by Cecil Wulfson, Claude Duval and Cecil Margot had three Dakotas, or C47's as they were more commonly known as. Their crews were made up of a Captain, Co-Pilot, Engineer, Radio operator and a Stewardess.

Some of the aircraft had very uncomfortable bucket seats either in the normal cross fuselage configuration or lined lengthways in the main fuselage. These usually accommodated about nineteen passengers. The normal configuration was not too popular with the Israeli Air Force. It was inconvenient taking the seats out when they 'borrowed' our planes.

On the stop overs in Israel, the crews took a few days off for rest and recreation between trips, and the aircraft were taken away, ostensibly for 'servicing'. They were then used by the Israel Air Force (IAF) as night bombers.

I recall on one of these Rest and Recreation weekends the crew decided to go into Tel Aviv for the weekend. At this time there were two Dakotas in Israel, including my favourite ZS-BYX. Over the weekend one of the aircraft was co-opted by the IAF to bolster their night bombing capabilities. When we returned to Haifa at the end of the weekend both aircraft were parked up but a tyre on one of them was badly gashed. It had picked up some shrapnel on a bombing mission over the Gaza strip. Since it was impossible to fly with the tyre in that condition, it presented us with a problem, considering the safety of crew, passengers and the aircraft. However, the air force came to the rescue and located a spare tyre in reasonable good condition in some small out of the way airfield, Ein Shemen, hardly a dot on the map. Our serviceable "Dak" was duly dispatched to uplift the spare tyre. It was about a twenty-minute flight from Haifa to an airfield that was an apology for an aerodrome, with a grass landing strip and a ramshackle control tower. Surprise! The Drome Manager was my old friend from University days, Victor Katz.

My first flight experiences

I received a call from Zuckerman who told me I was to join a PAAC DC-3 flight as a super-numery radio operator, which would allow me to obtain my flight time and my licence.

We took off from Palmeitfontein early in the morning of August 10th with Captain Alf Lindsay and carrying 22 volunteers. We flew up to Nairobi, then on to Khartoum, where I was surprised to meet Joe Friedman. Joe had worked at Rand Radio with Mendy and me before leaving for Israel a few months before us.

Our flight continued to El Adem where we logged our flight plan to Rome. After an hour's flight we changed direction for Haifa where we arrived on August 14th. Four days later we were heading for Europe where we would exchange planes and return to Haifa with South African volunteers. I made several of these flights with PAAC which included landings in London, Rome, Paris, Geneva, Zurich, Nicosia, Croydon and Prague.

Finally, back in South Africa, I presented my log book, with 200 hours flying time to the PMG, and my license as Air Radio Operator was confirmed.

Some of crew I flew with were Captain Harry Creed, Syd Excel, Jock Hamilton, Honniball, Dell Webb and Nobby Clark, Captain Alf Lindsay and Claude Duval. Syd became a folk hero, fighting bureaucracy. Having unfairly lost his flying licence, he stormed into the office of the Director of the Civil Aviation Authority and threatened the unfortunate individual with a Smith and Wesson six shooter. It brought to light many dubious practices and Syd was re-instated.

Apart from shuttling young South African Mahalnicks to Israel, we took on charter work and mail contracts, which I daresay was very profitable. We also carried paying civilian passengers from Israel to Europe and England. We had a monopoly at that time, considering that scheduled airlines were reluctant to enter areas of war conflict.

Our route up Africa took four tedious days and sometimes five, depending on weather conditions and mechanical problems. Some of our refuelling stops and night stops along the way were: Palmeitfontein (Johannesburg), Bulawayo, Lusaka, Ndola, Kasama, Tabora, Nairobi, Kisumu, Ntebbe, Juba, Malakal, Khartoum, and then our last stop in Africa, Wadi Halfa El Adem. After this we would head east across the Red Sea, Gulf of Aquaba and north to Haifa. Some of the places we linked up with in Europe were Nicosia in Cypress, Athens, Rome, Paris, Prague, London and Geneva.

In comparison with today's highly sophisticated satellite navigational systems and radio communications, we were stumbling around in the 'crystal set' era. All the work I did as a radio operator was in the Morse Code medium. The only time voice radio was used was by the pilot and co-pilot when in the range of a few miles from our destination.

On a flight over Africa, when the captain called for a position fix or barometric pressure and weather report, all we could pick up on our antiquated transceivers was Static. Operating aircraft compasses, over desert areas, were notoriously unreliable due to unknown magnetic forces over other territories. With the result that half the time we were flying we would be guessing and praying.

Most of the time the cloud was on the deck (at ground level). There was no way one could map read for lakes, railway tracks or roads. We would be flying around in the mist with not a clue where we were. The fuel indicators would be touching the dangerously low-level mark, the radio straining like mad to pick up the faintest signal from outer space, to establish some form of sanity between the ire of the captain and the radio operator. It was not very conducive to good inter crew relationships.

In one instance, we overshot our destined airport. It was by the sheerest luck, and the instincts of a good commander, who turned us around. As we landed the engine cut out, starved of gasoline.

With non-existent instrument landing systems and poor navigational aids across Africa, we would night stop all the way up. We usually made our last stop at about three or four o'clock in the afternoon and checked into a hotel with all the passengers. We would then take all the lads and lasses for a sight-seeing trip through the town, market places and other places of interest.

We owe a debt to the PAAC pilots who served us beyond the call of duty. They flew night and day, leaving the Central African airfields at sunrise and reaching their destination at the end of the following day.

Usually crews were up by 3am and out to the airport to service and complete the daily inspection on the aircraft. By 5am the passengers and luggage were loaded and off we went. Flying conditions over Africa, especially in the tropics, was a very uncomfortable affair. We flew at low altitude, which with no pressurisation in the cabin and turbulence being a daily occurrence, resulted in many sick passengers. On one occasion we were not able to go around a tremendous thunderhead, and had no option but to go through the cumulus nimbus. With disastrous results. The aircraft literally cartwheeled with the down and up drafts of the storm throwing us about 1000 metres each way.

One of the most unusual sights I ever saw and, according to the crew who had logged thousands of hours, was a phenomenon known as St. Elmo's Fire. It was a ball of fire, literally rolling from one wing tip, across the cockpit to the other wing tip and then just vanishing into thin air. Most frightening! Something very few have the privilege of experiencing.

Mendy and the Avro Anson

Mendy and Tittlestad took off from Wonderboom airport on their long haul up Africa to Israel. I left on my first flight with PAAC (Pan African Air Charter) about a week later. Our first night stop was Nairobi, Kenya. I had been told by the Federation to meet Mendy Vons and Tittlestad on my arrival, give them their funds and provide a report to the Federation and the Israeli Air Force.

When I stepped out of the Dakota onto the landing strip, who was there waiting to meet me? Mendy Vons, the Macher[ii]. He related their very eventful trip from South Africa to Nairobi, with a stopover in Bulawayo, a week earlier. Amongst the many problems they encountered was the external propeller driven generator, which supplied power to the radio transceiver. This unfortunately came adrift from its fittings and during its free flight, gravity motivated, to terra-firma, and gashed the side of the aircraft fuselage and rear ailerons.

The prop driven generator was not a standard fitting on Avro Anson's, as supplied to the Royal Air Force and South African Air forces. We believed that the previous owner of this particular aircraft, from whom the Zionist Federation bought it, came up with this bright idea to solve a thorny problem with their electricals and had one of the local bicycle mechanics do the installation.

Another problem encountered was the Heath Robinson supplementary fuel supply tanks which, at altitude, did not meet our expectations. Air locks developed in the rubber tubing that delivered the fuel to the main supply tanks. What we did not know in those days was that high-octane aviation fuel corroded rubber, which left a sediment that clogged up delicate mechanisms such as those required to drive variable screw propellers; which in turn helped the aircraft to maintain healthy altitudes.

The hydraulic systems also failed, which meant that the crank handle had to be turned one hundred and thirty-six revolutions to lower the undercarriage. Heavy work for the biceps. Unlike the B17, which can land quite safely with the undercarriage retracted into the fuselage, the Avro Anson did not have that capability.

So, there it was, an old WW2 training aircraft careering through the African skies without radio communication and with the attendant lack of pin-point 'fixing' facilities with ground stations; total cloud cover so no visual navigation aided by roads, railway lines and antiquated schoolboy maps.

Mendy and I took a stroll out to the Anson, which was parked out of sight close to the airport boundary fence. What a sorry mess! The fence was the common boundary with the Kenyan game reserve. You can hear the roar of lions and trumpeting of the elephants most nights. However, there must have been an odour from the fabric covering of the Anson which was appealing to Hyenas. They had squeezed through the security fencing and ripped the fuselage covering to ribbons! The old 'Annie' was a write-off and therefore abandoned by Mendy and Tittlestad, who took the first south bound ride back home. The skeletal remains were a silent reminder of the guts and determination of the few who were prepared to risk their lives in this battle.

Joe Friedman's Nightmare

On an overnight stop in Khartoum, we met one of our southbound aircraft night stopping at the same place. We met up with the passengers and crew at the hotel and I bumped into one of my friends, Joe Friedman. He had only just gone up to Eretz (Israel) and I enquired from him, "Joe, for heaven's sake, what are you doing here?"

This was his story. He was crewing on a Dakota night bombing mission. With the doors open there was a hurricane draft of wind through the fuselage. One of the young Israeli bomb throwers accidentally tripped on the rip cord of a parachute which was stowed up front. The velocity of the wind snatched the main chute out of the bag, billowing it out into the fuselage, and out of the bomb bay door. Visualise what that did to the aerodynamics of the plane. With great difficulty the crew instinctively took counter actions to right the aircraft, which was being dragged in a spiral dive down to disaster. Finally, a knife was found to cut the shrouds. Joe was, by his own admission, a total nervous wreck after that calamitous experience. The Pilot was one of the finest Dakota pilots in the world, Cyril Katz.

Asian Antics

Without exception our passenger compliment was always one hundred percent capacity. At Nairobi an Indian couple with two young children implored our captain to take them as far as Entebbe. Reluctantly he agreed, when two of our intrepid passengers consented to give up their seats and strap-hang in the aisle. We had been airborne for about an hour when a queue started to build up outside the only toilet. When things started to become desperate the air hostess banged on the door, requesting the occupant to hurry and give the others a chance. Finally, the door opened, and our Indian passenger nonchalantly made his exit. In his hands was a burning primus stove on top of which was a big pot, emanating therefrom the most delicious aroma of curried stew. Being very religious, and Halal, he had prepared a meal for his family.

They disembarked at Entebbe as planned and we took off for our next port of call. To our irritation a terrible smell started permeating throughout the plane. On searching the cabin, we finally came across a paper packet under one of the seats previously occupied by our Indian friends. They did not want to use our non-Halal toilets and preferred to squat, which one of them did into a paper packet. Instead of flushing it away, they decided it was to leave it in the main cabin. Obviously, a warped sense of humour!

Out of Africa

As well as shuttling young South African Mahal to Israel, some were also taken to Europe for the sake of convenience. Robbie Lowenberg, who was with us in 69th Squadron, recalled to me a time when he was dropped off in Italy with other young South Africans. They were herded on to an old unseaworthy tramp steamer in the south of Italy with Jewish Holocaust survivors from all over the continent, on their perilous journey to Israel. Sleeping on the deck with poor food and sanitation, medical students did their best to contain the outbreak of diarrhoea and whooping cough, which was endemic with the babies.

Many of these migrant boats were apprehended by the Royal Navy and diverted to Cyprus where passengers and crew would be herded into British concentration camps. They were held in squalid conditions in the extreme heat of the Middle East summers with extremely cold, damp wintery nights.

The young men that escaped the blockades went from the beaches straight into the army, where many lost their lives fighting Arabs, after having survived the Holocaust.

Masai Mania

Our night stops were friendly affairs with captain and crew dining together with the passengers. Our Captain told us that the next night stop was to be Tanganyika in Masai country. The Masai tribe have the tallest people in the world. Many of the men are over seven feet tall. The Captain went on to remark that they had penises to match. Much to the amusement of us all, one of the young women passengers we had on board, exclaimed "Yes Please! Can we see them?"

In fact, we did make a special point to go and see the Masai men. The male teenagers had weights, which were stones, attached to their penis to lengthen them. The Masai are cattle breeders and their main diet was a mixture of blood and milk. They would obtain the blood by bleeding one of the arteries of the animal. According to expert dieticians this was a very balanced diet, rich in protein. Whilst one herdsman was milking the cow another was syphoning blood from an artery of the same animal.

For most of our young volunteers this trip was the first time they had ever left the borders of South Africa. Everything around them was an experience of a lifetime. Usually after their sightseeing trip to the village markets they would come back to the plane loaded with souvenirs. Despite warnings, death masks, carvings of ivory, straw hats and the most useless trivia would be the order of the day and usually when landing in Israel most of it was left behind for the crew to dispose of.

Early one morning, a lady kept our aircraft waiting for half an hour when her friend advised the crew, just as we were about to take off, that she had gone back to the market to pick up a piece of ethnic jewellery she decided she could not live without. If her friend had not shed half a litre of tearful pleadings our Captain would have left her behind.

Behind the Iron Curtain

The trip to Prague was during the times when Czechoslovakia was under Communist domination. The trip was primarily to pick up some young Israelis. They had been put into detention and held there following one of the previous flights to uplift spares for Messerschmitt's, Spitfires and the flying Fortresses.

Apparently, they withheld information about hard currency, such as dollars and English pounds they had in their possession, which should have been declared on entering the country and noted in their passports. This they failed to do and going through passport control on their way out they were bodily searched and found to be in possession of this 'illegal' money. Due to the lengthy legal proceedings involved they had to be left behind.

I remember that one lad had bought a motor scooter, which had presented a real problem in loading and stowing in the cargo hold. Most of the crew usually brought holdalls stuffed with salamis, chocolate and rice, all for resale back in Eretz. Considering the shortage of these basic food items in Israel they had no problem finding willing customers at exorbitant prices. It was very enterprising and very profitable for those young entrepreneurs. Another well sought-after item was tea. I know of one crewman who eventually bought a small villa in Spain from these transactions – Kayn Aynhoreh (God Bless Him).

Home Comforts

When I started flying with Pan African Air Charter in early 1948 throughout most of the countries we flew to everything was heavily rationed. In England and Czechoslovakia, as air crew we were issued with very generous food ration coupons, which we would exchange for meat, tea, candy, butter and so forth. When we flew out the ground crews were on to us like a pack of wolves, begging us for left-over coupons.

In Israel, as flying crew, we had very special privileged food rations. Eggs imported from Poland, rice (albeit full of weevils), meat and so forth. If I remember correctly, our monthly pay was Five Israeli pounds, but South Africans were well looked after by the Zionist Federation. We received food parcels from home containing chocolates, biscuits and a brand of cigarettes 'Five Star', which none of us had ever heard of back home. Still, smokes were hard to come by in those days and we would puff on any old gasper, short of camel dung!

On the subject of remuneration, we South Africans were drawing a pittance, which didn't bother us at all. In fact, we would have willingly as volunteers been happy without any mazuma[iii] at all, deeming it a privilege just to be there. The non-Jewish, Swedish, English and American mercenaries were drawing, back home, $3000 (US Dollars) per month.

Joy Stick Jockeys

The flying scene in those days was extremely stressful with the continued lack of navigational aids and poor instrument landing systems. Winter and even in summer, conditions were cloudy or misty with rain, smog and snow which made visibility non-existent, right down to the ground. Even over Africa and especially in central tropical areas, for thousands of kilometres one only infrequently caught glimpses of the jungle beneath.

To give you an idea of how the stress and tensions affected my metabolism. For a period of three weeks my bowels refused to move. What amazed me was that I didn't feel constipated, despite eating three full meals a day, with snacks continually being served by the air hostess. Dining was at all hours of the day and late-night Suppers would be at 11, 12 and 1 o'clock in the morning after a long 15-hour stint in the air.

I remember one trip to France. Coming in to land at Orly airport, the weather was atrocious, gusty and misty with zero visibility. All the crew were up front on the flight deck, trying to spot some semblance of a break in the clouds, or the welcome sight of the landing lights. Involuntarily, in unison, we all let out shouts of horror. Sliding by, alongside of us, and looming into the heavens, was the Eiffel Tower! Had we connected, this would have been a disaster of the highest magnitude.

When we finally touched down at Orly airport the mother of all interrogations, regarding our movements, followed. Reports came in to the control tower of a renegade aircraft flying like crazy through the Parisian skies. Short of accusing us directly, it was inferred that we were the culprits. Naturally we disclaimed all knowledge of such a monstrous allegation!

Pastoral Pleasures

In England, our base of operation was a little known, out of the way, aerodrome by the name of Blackbush. It was very rustic, out in the countryside, close to Sandhurst Military College. The village had the most wonderful pub where air crew from all over the world congregated for their favourite tipple, which led to the most outrageous tales of their flying experiences. Croydon was also an airport well used in those days.

In due course, I did my last flight back to South Africa and submitted my logbook to the Civil Aviation Authority. After an impatient wait of some weeks, the Post Master General issued me with the valued official radio operator's licence. Certified to fly anywhere in the world and recognised by all airlines. I believe I must have been the youngest of the Mahal air crew. Certainly, the only one with an officially recognised CAA licence.

I was by now champing at the bit, waiting to get back to Israel and into action. I hounded Phil Zuckerman at the Federation offices every day, nagging to get on to the next flight with PAAC. I was finally booked on a flight, as a super-numery crew, with the captain's understanding that I would disembark at Haifa.

A Rude Awakening

A young woman's dream of the glamorous life of an air hostess was quickly shattered after the first few hours in the air, in a vibrating, noisy, badly ventilated, bucking, drafty ex South African Air Force C47 Dakota. The hostesses got on board at Palmeitfontein, looking chic, well-groomed and attractive in their blue uniforms. But after being on their feet day and night for four days, feeding twenty passengers, being at the beck and call of the four air crew members at all hours, being nauseous and air sick much of the time while dealing with vomiting passengers, soon took the glamour out of soaring into the romantic world of aviation.

Those poor Tsatskes (Kugels[iv]) aged very quickly. As crew we always found many young wonderful passengers who were willing to give us a hand dishing out food packages, prepared at each of our night stop hotels as a service and at a cost. South African, Beryl Aliasov had the distinction of being the first air hostess with El Al Israeli Air Line.

Last touch-down as a civilian

We landed at Haifa and as usual were met on landing by our agent, Hans Weisbrod, whom I'd met on previous flights. Quietly on the side, I mentioned to him that I was on my way to Tel Aviv to join the Israeli Air Force and would he organise a ride for me. He was surprised at this, and that I was even Jewish. I showed him my official papers, issued by the Federation, and the next morning at the crack of dawn I was on my way to Lydda[v] airport (as it was known in those days) in an Israeli Air Force Piper cub (we called them Piperschimdts). The Israelis used them to fly silently over Arab trenches. The pilot with one hand on the joystick, the other hand industriously tossing out hand grenades.

Induction Blues

My instruction, upon arrival in Israel, was to report to a distribution camp named Sarafand. On landing at Lydda one of the young ground crew took me in hand and arranged a lift for me in a Jeep. Weaving in and out of chaotic traffic we headed through the winding streets of Tel Aviv and finally to Jaffa, where Sarafand camp was situated. This was in the heart of the old Arab quarter adjoining Tel Aviv. At the start of hostilities Egyptian propaganda, hysterically, warned the Arab population living in Israel, notable in Haifa, Jaffa and other small villages, that they must flee from their homes as they would be slaughtered by the Jews.

The area of Sarafand covered a few city blocks and was security fenced. There were quite a number of high rise blocks of flats (apartments) in this area, and young recruits coming in from all over the world were garrisoned in comparative comfort, whilst in transit to their regiments.

Air Force headquarters in Tel Aviv was based in an hotel commandeered by the military, in Hayarkon street, aptly named the Hayarkon Hotel. I had kept in close touch with my old buddy, Mendy Vons, and by the time I arrived for induction he had already been in the country for a couple of months. Together we arrived at the Hayarkon for my interview. Although security was pretty tight at the entrance Mendy, who had a blustery way about him, coupled with chutzpa[vi] galore, charmed the young security guard into waving us through to the inner sanctum of sanctums, despite us not having the necessary magical papers to enter.

My posting; at last.

The crew placement officer of the air force, at that time, was a lovely lass by the name of Elsie Ben Yehuda. She was the wife of Dov Ben Yehuda. They were both South Africans. Dov was very high up in the hierarchy, together with Smoky Simons, being experienced navigators and administrators with the South African Air Force during World War 2. Now the leading lights, together with others such as Danny Rosen, Cecil Margot and many others, were active in getting the fledging Israeli Air Force off the ground. Figuratively and literally.

We met up with Elsie and she wanted to know my full background, with regard to my flying experience and so forth. After taking copious notes, and Mendy prompting me from the background as he wanted me to fly with C46 Commandos in the Air Transport Command. They were mainly concerned with uplifting war material in Europe for the Palmach and Air Force. At the end of the day, Elsie left the choice up to me. Either to join the ATC, or the

19

squadron of three B17 Flying Fortresses based at the old RAF base, at Ramat David. I had no hesitation in deciding on the Flying Forts. The main reason was in light of my experience doing charter flying in Europe.

Don't start the war without me.

I was duly posted to Ramat David Air Force base, where I joined the 69th Squadron which comprised of three B17 Flying Fortresses. I was replacing crew member Joe Behr from Krugersdorp as radio operator/air gunner. He took me in hand, to show me the ropes on the radio equipment, how to set the antennae and how to 'swing the compasses'. Flying over desert areas played havoc with the magnetic fields associated with compasses.

The base was built by the British for the Royal Air Force located in the Middle East. It was well set up with Nissen huts for the personnel, workshops, hospital, operational headquarters, dining facilities and concrete revetments, where we parked our aircraft under camouflage netting. This base was shared with the 103 Dakota Squadron, and sundry other small aircraft.

The B17s were bought and the squadron assembled in Czechoslovakia and were to be flown non-stop to Israel. It was decided, in order to get as much mileage out of the trip as possible, to bomb some targets in Egypt on the way home. The aircraft were duly bombed up, and the loads were dropped on Cairo and, I think, Alexandria.

In this way this made aeronautical history. In this bombing mission, neither the aircraft nor the crew, had ever been to the country for which they fought. Thereafter there were many missions over Egypt.

We did three or four bombing raids a day over El Arish. The flak was intense. In our crew we had our navigator-bombardier Syd Kentridge from

Cape Town, a young Dane, Chris Jurgen Christensen, who was a hired professional. He would arm our bombs just before the target spot. Several times we had 'hang-ups' where the bombs would fail to drop when the trigger was pulled. Jurgen would kick away at these recalcitrant bombs and when he had no luck he would call us over to hang from the spars and join him in kicking until they fell loose and dropped.

Fly-Past Celebrations

Our Flying Fortresses were named the 69th Squadron, code named "The Hammers", and based initially at Ramat David. No doubt named after Kibbutz Ramat David which bordered our airfield. Also close by was the Moshav Gvat. These two farming communities specialised, at that time, in milk, chicken and turkey production. Whenever we had a bit of free time, some of us lads used to visit the dairy at milking time, and, at the invitation of the friendly kibbutzniks, used to gorge ourselves with the cold fresh milk flowing down the cooling coils of the milking apparatus. At times we even used to help the young lasses in the huge hen house batteries, housing I believe up to fifty thousand birds.

Moshav Gvat raised turkeys for the table in a very big way. I recall, after hostilities had ended and the United Nations voted for the establishment of the state of Israel, we decided to have a celebratory parade at the base with a band and a march past, with the Chens (Women Commandos) and all personnel. The main feature was to be a fly-past of B17's buzzing the air field. According to Kenny Jacobson, one of our crew, the aircraft came in so low that the bandstand collapsed. It was only the following day that we heard that thousands of turkeys on Moshav Gvat had died of fright. Turkeys are very sensitive birds, and the tremendous roar of the engines had killed them. The air force received a hefty bill to settle.

Flying Doctors

We were not altogether in the bad books at the kibbutz. An epidemic of whooping cough broke out amongst young infants at the kibbutz and the moshav. A medical expert advised that if it were possible to take them up to a very high altitude, they would be cured. I vaguely remember our crew taking the babies, all bundled up warmly, to about 10 000 feet. I do not recall whether reports were later received as to the efficacy of the experiment.

Recreation

The air crew of the 69th were issued with new, American Air Force, heavily zipped, olive green bomber jackets, fur lined with wool based collars. Our mess committee designed a baseball cap, in black with two white stripes. The lads of 103 Squadron, flying the Dakotas, had their own colour scheme. We also had a go at forming an American type football team.

Regretfully, our American buddies just could not instil in the South African, English and other nationalities, the intricacies of those unfathomable rules, where you tackled the guys without the ball. Eventually we settled for the European variety of football. We regularly played other teams on the base. To see the Americans in action was the most hilarious spectacle, as they also found it difficult to convert to our style of football. Rugby was an impossible exercise.

Encounters of another kind

We were a motley crew stationed at Ramat David, later transferred to Telnof (previously named Aquir), and we literally came from all corners of the globe. South Africans, English, Canadians, Americans, Russians, Indians (Abie Nathan, who in post war years became very well known for his peace missions to Egypt), Danish, Swedish, German, Polish and naturally many Israeli's. We were involved in a strange kind of war.

For weeks the flying missions would go on, day and night, in frenzied activity. The United Nations would get involved and a cease-fire would be invoked for a few weeks. We would then laze around all day, sunbathing, playing squash, gin rummy and klabberjas. Jerry Weinstein, our American bombardier, and inveterate gambler organised a gambling casino. Playing 24 hours round the clock, dice, canasta 21, roulette and other subtle ways of parting you from your hard-earned shekels.

On our free days off we would all dress up in our, newly issued, dark brown gabardine uniforms and take an air force bus, or hitch hike, in to Tel Aviv. Our favourite watering hole was a café called Gali Yam, on the beach front. Close by was a restaurant specialising in sea food. They had their own private pool with live fish, in abundance, swimming around. The diner selected his fish, the waiter caught it and from there, after preparation, straight into the frying pan.

You can imagine the condition our lads were in come nightfall, after an afternoon solid drinking, and I don't mean gazoz (a local fizzy soft drink)! I must admit, the South African lads were the wildest. Off to the fish pond, out in the street with absolutely no inhibitions, off came every stitch of clothing and into the pool they went to sober up. No need to relate what the restaurant management thought of these shenanigans. Nevertheless, they valued our patronage and reparations were the order of the day.

Wrong Airfield, Wrong Country

Our Flying Fortresses were only used for daylight bombing missions. Our maximum ceiling was in the vicinity of 14 000 feet, due to the fact that we had no oxygen facilities for higher altitudes, which the aircraft were easily capable of.

An incident I remember clearly, and on discussing it with Sid Seftel, our navigator, was surprised that, after fifty years, he also had total recall. On one of our missions, we were returning from a bombing raid over one of the many Egyptian targets. Our commander was John McConville, an American and a most beloved character. A real professional with a cauliflower ear which, I suspect, he got after connecting with the terra-firma, after being happily involved with the nightly monumental drinking sessions, which were the norm at the base mess.

We had made a lovely smooth landing, on what we presumed was the runway at Ramat David. We all heaved the usual sigh of relief at having made it back home, once again in one piece. The air gunners and I quietly looking out of the side bays, watching the revetments glide by. A jeep, with a number of armed soldiers on board, crept up alongside us, pacing us as we slowed down. On looking closer we noticed, to our amazement, Arab markings on the side panels of the vehicle. The driver and his passengers, one of whom was manning a Bren machine gun, nonchalantly cruising alongside us with rather pleasant expressions on their faces, as if to say this is a strange looking aircraft. Must be one of ours, but what the hell is it doing around here? In unison, I think we all realised the monumental blunder we had perpetrated. Mac slammed the four throttle levers hard up against the dash and, with the supercharged Wright Cyclone engines screaming in protest, we took off like a rocket, with the crew in the fuselage sprawling all over each other and hanging on for dear life. Hey Seftel, was this your mish-mosh[vii]?

Sid later recounted to me that, as Mac was landing, he asked him what he was doing landing here but, he seemed to want to put down. Sid thought it may have been to visit the fighter squadron, but he wasn't that sure and thought we were a bit close to the west bank border, and that as Mac touched down Sid yelled into the intercom that this was Arab territory.

I can imagine what the Arabs must have thought of this missed opportunity to bag a flat-footed duck. After months of trying to shoot us down with their sophisticated, electronically controlled, 88 calibre anti-aircraft guns over El Arish. Here we were, a sitting target, in their own back yard.

To prevent future crews flying with hangovers, and to obviate any further mishaps such as ours, the powers that be tried to enforce the rule "Twelve hours from bottle to throttle". I don't think this was met with any enthusiasm.

Air Minded Women's Society

Some of the good ladies in Haifa took it upon themselves to form this association. Basically, it was to entertain the air force men stationed at Ramat David. Invitations were extended to all us, via our Station Commander.

During lulls in our flying activities a roster was drawn up. It was usually an invite to Shabbat Friday night, and the roster identified who would be hosted, and by whom. For those interested a personnel carrier was laid on to take them to a central drop off point in Haifa. The host families would then pick us up and take us to their homes. I think that most of us went along for the home cooked food, Knaydl, Kreplach and Kichel[viii]. What Naches[ix]! Of course, we also went to meet the family, especially the daughters and other young attractive lassies that invariably were invited along to meet the fliers.

To be a TAYAS (Pilot/flier) in Israel in those days created some kind of mystique with the Israeli's. It was as if we were something akin to men from outer space. We were also invited to attend High Festivals, but I don't think any of us ever saw the inside of a shul. By the strangest co-incidence and for some inexplicable reason, on those particular days we were always on standby due to imminent resumption of hostilities. God forgive us. Eats, drinks and female company were all that we were interested in.

Squadron Mascot

Visiting Nazareth was a regular occasion. A load of heavy washing was taken in, usually every two weeks, by truck and the Arab laundries did the job for us. Nazareth was predominantly Arab and mostly very poor people who were Christian Arabs. The sewerage would run in surface canals in the middle of the street. It was pathetic to see the many blind children at their begging posts, the flies in their thousands, crawling all over their faces.

Once a month there would be a sale in the main square of sheep, goats and Arab horses. My mate, Jack Liponetsky, one of our American air gunners was mad about horses. On the pretence of being a buyer he had the privilege of being able to ride these horses.

On one of our strolls through the village, a ragged, flea bitten, tan puppy attached himself to us. We duly took him home with us and he became the squadron mascot. Naturally we named him 'Hammer'. We even made, with the help of one of our operations ladies, a nylon parachute, harness and all. With lots of T.L.C (tender, loving care) and grooming, he blossomed. Occasionally we would sneak him aboard and take him up with us on a test flight.

Secret Weapon

Some bright spark in operations, with nothing better to do with his time, thought up a smart idea to terrorise the Arab population. Plans were drawn up and this devilish device was constructed in our aeronautical workshop.

Basically, it was a construction of about five or so 44-gallon oil drums. The lids and bottoms were removed, and the drums were welded together, end to end. Holes were cut all around the drums, about 12 inches in diameter, along the full length and breadth of this long tube. Inside the tube a number of coloured lights were mounted. These were set to flash on and off and were powered by the electricals from the main fuselage of the B17. Also, on the outside of the tube was welded protuberances, designed to create wailing sounds as the apparatus was dragged at high speed through the atmosphere.

It was a major engineering feat to attach this lot, together with the winching apparatus, alongside the tail end of the fuselage. The king pin in the whole operation was tail-end Charlie, our rear end gunner. A young south African by the name of Stanley Nash. It was his job, when we arrived over target, to winch the tube out slowly until it got to the end of a fifty-foot tether.

The rest of the crew was selected to do this very unusual night flight and with old reliable John McConville, our commander, we took off. A few hours after sunset, on a moonless night, when darkness had well and truly set in, we headed for the Gaza strip. The intention was to fly over many of the small villages in the area, including our usual targets such as El Arish, Khan Younis, Rafah and so forth. As the Forts were only used in daylight bombing raids, the crew felt very uncomfortable in this strange environment. It was, at any rate, a good night training flight for our pilots.

Within half an hour we were over our destination and Mac gave Stan the go ahead to winch out slowly. This presented no problems, considering the aid of the slipstream. To be effective, we needed to do some low flying in order that our secret weapon be clearly seen and heard by those on the ground. Slashing through the desert skies at 180 miles per hour, it was very doubtful whether anybody saw us, let alone heard our sirens blasting out.

We cruised around for about an hour or so when Mac decided it was time to go home. He gave Stan instructions to winch the device back on board. Easier said than done! Whilst it was easy enough letting it out, it was, considering the slipstream, a physical impossibility to fish it back on board again. Despite two of us crawling in the narrow confines to help Stan, we reported to Mac that we were unsuccessful in hauling it back in. After due consideration by Mac, he quietly set course for the Mediterranean and gave us instructions to cut the cable and ditch it in the ocean. At our post operation briefing we concluded that the exercise was an 'Unqualified Failure'.

Taking into consideration that it involved the lives of ten crew, a valuable aircraft and with questionable benefits, it was meshugga[x] (Madness).

Sick Bay Survivor.

During a lull in one of the United Nations truce negotiations I woke up one morning with a headache and sore throat, which in a few hours developed into a cold. Not long after, it developed into the mother of all influenza's. I took to my bunk and, after a few days of taking proprietary medications, it was obvious to my buddies that I was seriously unwell. We had a sick bay in the lower camp of the RD AFB, close to the Chens (Women's Auxiliary) sleeping quarters.

My mates obtained permission from the commander to have me checked in. Having not eaten for a few days and being continually in a cold sweat, I was in a state of 'non-compos mentis'. I vaguely remember being attended to by a young doctor at the camp hospital, if one could euphemistically call it that, and being visited by Jack the Lip and Robbie Lowenberg. Sometime thereafter I vaguely recall the sound of explosions. I was later informed that the lower camp was the recipient of errant bombs, dropped by the Egyptian Air Force, and intended for the revetments, where our B17's and other aircraft were parked.

When I finally started coming around, I found that I was being nursed by a young South African nurse, Sarah Witt. She was seconded to our base and, according to the story she told me, when she arrived she took one look at me and decided I was on my last legs due to the ravages of double pneumonia. On checking with the 'doctor' as to what medication he had prescribed for me, he blithely informed her that I had a bad cold and he was pumping me full of aspirins and cough mixture. I am convinced that had Sarah Witt arrived a day later, I would not be telling this tale today. With antibiotics, penicillin and the right medication administered by my guardian angel, I soon recovered my consciousness.

I seemed to have had an abnormal number of visits from my friend Robbie during that time. It was only many years later, at the time of writing this book, and in conversation with Kenny Jacobson that the reason became very clear to me. Robbie had a crush on Sarah! Sadly, Robbie Lowenberg died a few years after my hospital trip, at a very young age.

Sarah instigated an inquiry into the credentials of the 'doctor'. He was a young Englishman, by profession a ladies hairdresser from Piccadilly Circus, who had fraudulently passed himself off as a qualified doctor. Needless to say, he was summarily dismissed. I don't know what his eventual fate was but perhaps this 'schemdrik' was court martialled and maybe sent to the trenches!

Gunnery Lessons

Our gunnery instructor was an ex Royal Australian Air Force officer, Jack Garbasz. He was small in stature but a genius in his profession.

The armour on the B17's was replaced with Browning 500's, which were very difficult to cock, especially for puny little guys like myself. Jack taught us the correct technique, how to strip them whilst blindfolded and all the various aspects of gunnery to do with trajectories etc.

The Flying Forts we flew had all the hydraulically operated turrets removed. Top, bottom, side and even tail end Charlies (tail gunners) were removed. Simple frameworks were installed, to limit the movements of the Browning machine guns, so that we didn't shoot our own wing tips and tail ends off.

Each aircrew was issued with a side arm. Usually Italian Barretta's. The pistols each had a clip of six cartridges. Our instructions "If you get shot down and survive, shoot five Arabs and save the sixth shot for yourself". No prisoners were taken by the enemy. Before slitting your throat, they did the most unspeakable mutilations to your manhood so that in the afterlife you would be unable to produce an heir!

A day in the life

Butch Bottger, an ex SAAF veteran and a Christian was affectionately renamed Butch Ben Yok. His Hebrew name literally translated meant 'the Son of Christian'. Butch was attached to 103 Squadron also based at Ramat David, flying Dakotas converted to bombers for night time operations. Our Flying Fortresses were capable of higher altitudes and were used for day time bombing missions only.

Butch and his crew made their last landing long before dawn. After dispersal and a light breakfast Butch would take great delight in crashing his way into our Nissen huts whilst ringing a large brass bell. The ear-piercing peels were meant to arouse us from the previous evenings hangovers.

In summer our beds were protected with mosquito nets from the enormously large and strong breed of mosquitos found in Israel. We were also advised to check our boots for scorpions and other creepy crawlies before putting them on. When getting into bed at night we were again advised to shake out our blankets to remove any unwelcome sleeping companions.

Winter nights were bitterly cold, and we slept in our long johns, flying overalls with every other bit of clothing we could find over the blankets for added warmth. Balaclavas were worn to protect your face. Our Nissen huts, bequeathed to us by the RAF, had no heating. They had been left behind when the British forces pulled out of Israel. When they left, their military installations were stripped by the Arabs before they too abandoned them.

After being rudely awoken by Butch, we would assemble in our flying gear outside our quarters where we would then board an old bus, draped in olive green camouflage. We would rush for a seat and leave the rest to stand. The bus drivers were a wild bunch and would roar off at break neck speed to the cheder ochel (dining room) for an early morning breakfast. We had more traffic casualties in our camp than in the whole of the war zone.

Breakfast would be salted herrings, labinier (Yoghurt), boiled eggs, rye bread, green olives, gefilte fish, cheese and hot coffee without sugar. Not good fare for an empty stomach after a night out. Some of us never did get used to it, whilst others thrived on it.

Jack Liponetsky, from Brooklyn, enjoyed it so much he would finish our leftovers. His appreciation was not for the faint hearted. He would let off steam from both ends! However, despite our initial disgust, we soon got used to it as he was such a loveable character. He was, what I imagined, a typical Chicago gangster look alike. Square jawed with the inevitable dark stubble, squat build, like a bull dog. A real Haimisher mensch (homely, warm and friendly person).

The mess staff and kitchen were on duty 24 hours a day. Aircrew, operational personnel, technicians and mechanics from the various squadrons coming and going at all hours of the night and day. Our flying crew had special privileges regarding the menu, much to the disgust of the ground personnel. We were allowed rations of meat, eggs, rice (with weevils) and imported cheese. No doubt to go some way in compensation for the stress and drain on our mental and physical reserves.

After a hasty breakfast, back into the bus, and within a few minutes we screamed to a halt alongside the revetments, where our three 'Forts' were lined up. The ground crew fussed around us like a gaggle of broody hens. With a pull from the first man in, and a push from your buddy behind, we all clambered aboard.

Our crew usually consisted of nine men. The Captain John McConville (Mac); co-pilot Issy Noach (South African); navigator Sid Seftel (South African); flight engineer Bill Wadman (Canadian), bombardier Jerry Weinstein (USA), armourer Jurgen Christensen (Denmark); radio operator Zan Swartzberg (South African); tail-end-Charlie Stanley D Nash (South African); and two waist gunners Yeki Robinson (German) and Kenny Jacobson (South African). Our crew were mostly Jewish with the exception of Mac, Chris and Bill. Issy (nicknamed Zayde – grandfather) was the oldest Mahal flier in the IAF and I was the youngest. Our Crew bonded well together and became a team. Learning all about each other's foibles and becoming comfortable with each other.

All aboard! Our Captain, with the help of the external auxiliary battery pack, would splutter the engines into life, one by one. Revving them up to a tremendous roar and resultant bone shaking vibrations.

Chocks Away!

Off we crept to our point of departure as the first rays of light peeped over the horizon. With ten minutes left we undertook our pre-take-off checklist with strictly no radio communication with air traffic control. Up would go the green 'VERY' light signalling the all clear to take off. Each aircraft would have a different target and over the intercom we would hear McConville shouting "Guys, brace yourselves for take-off. We are on our way to El Arish". Oi Strak (Oh, fear) and groans all around.

Inching our way onto the main runway, each pilot had a hand on two throttle levers, twitching them slowly up, winding the engines up to maximum revolutions; the propellers a solid blur. Everything chaffing at the bit and, even with our helmets on, a deafening roar.

Off went the brakes and with a jerk, like a pebble out of a slingshot, we are on our way. At eighty knots the tail lifts, at 120 knots we ride along on the big front wheels. Suddenly at 140 knots of speed there is no vibration. We are airborne. Wing flaps up and at 200 feet altitude it's safe enough to retract the undercarriage. Now we are free from land and slicing through the air.

The empty weight of our B17 was around ten tons, with fully laden fuel tanks and a pay load of four thousand pounds we would have a range of 3000 miles. As our targets were not more than 300 miles away we kept our fuel supply to the minimum with a small reserve for emergencies. This let us load our bomb bays with a few extra hundred pounds of TNT.

The most vulnerable area of the plane was where the turret had been removed, just above the flight deck. With the turret removed we carried one less gunner and, as a result, when over target the radio operator and navigator stood by as gunners.

The distance for today's target of El Arish was approximately two hundred miles from Ramat David and with our airspeed of 180 mph we would be over our target in about an hour. Our Fort had a climb rate of 1000 foot per minute so within twenty minutes we would be at our maximum ceiling of fourteen thousand feet. Above that we would need a supplementary oxygen supply, which we did not have.

On this occasion we were flying alone instead of the usual configuration of three. There would be less chance of being knocked out of action by anti-aircraft fire as we would be a smaller target and less likely to be spotted by enemy fighter planes. It also meant that our bombing mission would be three targets, spreading the enemy air force thin. One disadvantage however, was that our payload over the target area was diminished and sparsely spread.

I get myself organised at my communications nook, which is a small space, hard up against the main bulkhead of the flight deck. On the right hand side I get a good view of the starboard engines through a small window. I have limited vision, but I can, nevertheless, keep a wary eye open for enemy fighter planes. At my feet, where I can almost touch them with my toes, are the ten lethal 500-pound bombs. They sit there like peas in a pod, dangling from their shackles.

I am listening out on a frequency tuned to our operations command post back at Ramat David, monitoring for any information or recall due to exceptional circumstances. Perhaps the Arabs have declared peace again? I am wondering who is on radio duty today? Is it one of the terrible twins, Mokkie Wies or Aubrey Wassyng (both South Africans from Johannesburg)?

Ten minutes into the mission I hear Mac on the intercom to the gunners. "Check your guns". I hear the sharp cracks from Yeki and Kenny as they cocked the Browning. Then, the clatter as they let off a burst. You can feel the stutter vibrating the main frame and I watch the tracers through my window, spinning away harmlessly. Kenny reports to the Captain on the intercom "Port waist gun functional", followed by Yeki "Starboard waist gun functional". Stan to Mac, "Tail gun functional".

Mac is being very loquacious today and announces on the intercom to the crew, "remember guys, keep a sharp eye open. For the next thirty minutes the fighter planes you see are ours"!

We have the lads from 101 Squadron on escort duty today. They have a limited endurance and don't want to mess around over the target, with shrapnel whizzing around.

I am wondering to myself which of the flyboys (fighter pilots) are looking after us today. Could it be Ezer Weizman (who went on to become President of Israel), or American ace, Slick Goodlin?

As I twiddle the knobs on the communications receiver I hear, through static, strong distinctive South African accents speaking Afrikaans. Could it be the two Cohens? Syd from Odendaalsrust, or Jack from Cape Town? Or, maybe Rolfe Futerman from Durban, or Denny Wilson an ex-RAF pilot during World War 2, who was offered the post as flight instructor with the Egyptian Air Force to train their fighter pilots.

When the hostilities began between the Israelis and the Arabs, Denny decided that his sympathies lay with the Israelis. He quietly packed his bags and slipped across the border to join us. In one of the dog fights with the enemy, Denny shot down one of their fighter planes. He told us that he knew the pilot, who had been one of his former students. He told us that the pilot had made exactly the same mistakes in combat as he did in training and it was those mistakes that led to his ultimate loss.

Thirty minutes into the mission Chris, the Dane, straddled the bombs and started arming them. Chris was tall, good looking, blonde and brown as a berry from sunbathing. I watch his fingers and hands, the skin on the backs of his hands peeling and leaving white blotches, industriously snipping off the safety wire clamps. These hold the little propellers which protrude a few inches outside the nose of the bomb. He gives the prop a twirl on its shaft, just to make sure it turns freely. The principle is that when the bomb is released,

36

the draft, as it falls, turns the propeller so that the shaft impregnates into the detonating mechanism of the bomb, exploding it on impact.

We are well into the mission now and the escorts have left us on our own. Priority number one! Keep your eyes open for enemy aircraft. I hear Syd advising Mac of our expected arrival time over target. Roger that! Not more than twenty minutes to go; Ten minutes' Mac instructs Syd to brief Jerry, the bombardier, with vital information such as ETA, air speed, wind speed, altitude and compass heading. Five minutes and Issy Noach warns Chris to stand clear. The bomb bay doors swing slowly wide open. A cold stream of air blasts into your face, the sound proofing goes to 'hades' and the wind noise is deafening.

Not long to go now, we can feel Mac weaving the Fort gently to and fro on final approach. This may just fool the anti-aircraft gunners. Wiley old fox! Up ahead you can see the grey puffs of smoke as the ack-ack shells explode. Right into our path now and it seems to be coming in on two different levels. Twelve thousand feet and fourteen thousand feet. Oy Vei is mir! (Oh, woe is me).

Seftel to Weinstein "ETA to target 2 minutes, 30 seconds, speed 185 mph, Altitude 13,500 feet, heading 235 degrees, drift 21mph, barometric pressure 0900 bars. Syd has done his duty and Jerry now instructs Mac over the intercom; "altitude OK, reduce revs a fraction, one degree left, hold steady".

By now we are in the thick of things. The puffs of smoke are all around us and we can clearly hear the sound of exploding anti-aircraft shells, woof, woof, woof, sounds like barking dogs. Yishkadal veyishkadas! (prayer for the dead)!

Weinstein is on his hands and knees crouching over the Norden bomb aimer. He is in the nose cone of the Fort and has the most beautiful view in the world, but he is oblivious to everything around him, except his task.

Concentrating deeply on the work in hand as we are into our final approach. "Half a degree to port, hold steady! Hold steady! That's it!! Jerry jabs the release on the bombsight, "Bombs Away"!

Chris and I are listening to all this on the intercom and are ready for the release of the payload, we stand with our legs astride the bomb bay. No parachutes on, no safety harness, and look down at El Arish, our target. Airfield, rail yards, petrol storage tanks, workshops, all five miles below us.

Soundlessly the bomb release mechanisms actuate, and the missiles fall away. They sway wildly, then stabilise as the tail fins grip into the thin air. We watch intently as the bombs drop, getting smaller and smaller until they vanish altogether from sight. We switch our gaze to the ground where little mushrooms of smoke sprout up all over the target area. "Well done Jerry. Spot on!"

Just then a shout from Chris, "Dammit, we have three hang ups". We were expecting this as it happens all the time. These are the bombs that fail to release. Two are on Chris's side and one on mine. With our slippered feet, we kick away at the offending loads of destruction. Chris manages to get one away. He keeps a chisel and hammer handy, for just such an occasion. He takes off his heavy woollen mittens and proceeds to attempt to dislodge the errant lumps, by slicing away the immovable shackles holding them firmly in their cradles.

The jammed release mechanisms are holding firm. He tries the one on my side, no luck. I read the writing on the bomb next to me and it states,

"Mazaltov". With my schoolboy Hebrew I know this means Good Luck. Well, no mazal (luck) for this baby; it's too late to keep trying. If we get it away now it may drop on the El Arish residential area, and that would create a gevalt (furious reaction) with the United Nations.

We don't have any worries about enemy fighters at this stage as they stay away from us lest they get knocked out of the skies by their own Anti-Aircraft ground gunners. Our vigilance wanes and all we focus on is the barrage complicating our dash for home. Usually when we have hang-ups we head out over the Mediterranean, where we take our time and jettison the unwelcome cargo over the ocean. This trip, we decide to take them home where the ground crew can evaluate the problem and get it sorted out once and for all.

The snag! Should we have a heavy landing, the chances of dislodging these lethal weapons on the tarmac would have tragic consequences. I have, in my kit, an emergency radio transmitter in case we have to crash land in the desert. With it comes a long antenna cable, about 100 feet long which is hoisted into the air by an orange coloured box kite. Chris and I use this to firmly lash the two remaining bombs securely to the shackles and the rigid framework of the bomb bay. With the doors closed we also have that little bit extra security.

With shouts of glee all around we leave the barking dogs behind and head home. "Vigilance guys, vigilance", from our Zayde (grandfather) Issy Noach.

We had been issued with flack suits to wear during our missions, but we never did wear them as they were heavy and uncomfortable. We just lay them on the floor of the aircraft next to our combat positions and stood on them for protection against flack. Our feet were very vulnerable, and we were not allowed to wear ordinary flying boots in case of accidental sparks, or static, igniting the volatile fuel or other combustible fumes. We were issued with lamb's wool lined slippers to wear so the flack suits gave us a certain amount of protection. In all our missions we only had one casualty. One of our crew, Wilf Jackson, a lad from England, got a hot lump of shrapnel up his tachis (bum)!

The next part of my job is to send a "Mission Completed" signal to air force headquarters. The code word for the day is "Masada". The acknowledgement comes back to me in Morse, "Message received". I recognise the operator by his 'fist'. Every radio operator has a distinctive style, like a person's handwriting or voice. "Thanks, Mokkie, over and out".

"Hey Zan, how about some music?" asks Issy. I roam around the wave bands and pick up some swinging jazz from Benny Goodman on the Voice of America. Happy days are here again!

We only did one mission that day and nobody complained. By the time the ground crew, with all the complications, removed the eggs that came home to roost, the sun was already high in the Holy Land Heavens. Maintenance in the dusty desert conditions of the Middle East was particularly vexing. With inadequate resources, high octane aviation fuel of not very high standard, it all created very time consuming and innovative mechanical procedures.

Our end of day task was to go over the Browning machine guns very carefully, stripping them, oiling the hundreds of bits and pieces, to ensure that in the heat of the moment, no failures would occur at critical times.

That was our day: A good day.

In the crew mess that evening we ate our supper and the 'tipple' is flowing freely. It is eight o'clock and we tune in to our favourite radio station; Radio Cairo. It was better than the Goon show with a laugh a minute.

The newsreader came on air and we all listened in.

"This is Radio Cairo and I am Gamors el Bulla Dusta, reading the news. This morning two hundred Israeli bombers raided El Arish. Fifty were knocked out of the sky by our anti-aircraft batteries. Eighty-five were shot down by our courageous heroes of the Egyptian Air Force and seventeen Israeli Spitfires were shot down. Our undefeated superior Egyptian bombers carried out raids on Haifa, Jerusalem and Tel Aviv. All our aircraft returned safely." End of Bulletin.

At the end of the Israeli War of Independence, according to Cairo statistics the Israelis lost three thousand heavy duty bombers and a thousand fighter planes!

The Widow Maker

On a morning towards the end of my tour of duty Robbie Lowenberg and myself were having a leisurely breakfast, whilst playing a hand of Klabiyas, a sort of two handed bridge game, evolved centuries ago in Eastern Europe. No young Jewish lads' education would be complete without a good working knowledge of the intricacies of this card game, where luck played very little help in the long run of this fascinating spell.

We had a number of young Yemenite lassies, WAAF's helping in operations. During our game one of our favourite WAAF's arrives at our accommodation with the message that our Wing Commander, an American by the name of Arnold Ilowite, wants to see me. Now, I wonder aloud, what do

41

you suppose this is all about. I arrive at his office at Operations and he sits me down.

"Zan, I believe you have an International Aeronautical radio operators licence?", "Yes, I have", I assure him. "Right, you're off to Italy to join a ferry back to Israel with an aircraft for our squadron". Arnold was a perfectionist and could not abide fools lightly. His favourite expression in Yiddish was to call them Schmegeges (fool)! (Later, when I was in New York in 1950, Arnold and his Dad would take me to my first baseball game).

The resident camp photographer took my photographs, which were immediately sent up to Tel Aviv and, within a few days, I was advised that my new Israeli passport was ready for uplifting.

Being on official business, a small Piper cub aircraft was laid on to whisk me away to Air Force headquarters in Tel Aviv. My passport was ready for me. (I often now regret that I did not keep this passport with the apartheid situation in South Africa).

A folder with my air ticket, instructions, addresses and phone numbers of my contacts in Rome and the magnificent sum of two hundred American Dollars, to cover hotel, meals, travelling and other minor expenses in Italy.

It was thought that I would spend no more than two nights on this trip. My flight was booked on Pan African Air Charter, with whom I had flown many hours, some pleasant and others not so pleasant. I was to take off from Lydda Airport and the flight would take me to Chiampino Airport, just outside Rome. The Captain on board was Nobby Clarke. It was like coming home, having flown with Nobby on a short leg with PAAC.

Nobby was an Englishman with a prominent nose. When I first met him, years ago, he asked me whether I was Jewish. I replied "Yes, I am too". I was a bit defensive in my response to the question, as I wondered why he would be asking this when he so clearly was Jewish too. It was only later that I found out he was not Jewish and was frequently mistaken to be so, due to his proboscis. There was always a bit of a prickly feeling between us after that.

The First Officer was a legendary figure, whom I had often heard about and now I was privileged to meet. At that time, he was a man in his sixties. Kurt Kay. He flew as a fighter pilot with the German Luftwaffe, in the Great War (World War One). He earned the Iron Cross First class, having shot down many Allied airmen in his tour of duty.

Boarding the Dakota, I was seated next to a young Israeli, with the most awful scars and disfigurements to his face and hands. He had been crew on one of those miniature little French tanks that the Israeli Army had acquired. The tank was hit by an Arab shell and he was the only survivor. He was on his way to England for plastic surgery.

Bella Italia

On landing at Chiampino Airport I was to meet up with my contact, Danny Agronsky. He practically lived at the airport and we had previously met when I flew with Pan African Air Charter. He was a trouble-shooter par excellence who spoke Hebrew and a dozen other European languages. He knew every minor and major official at Chiampino.

I was booked into the Hotel Massimo D'Azaglio, where other crew members for the ferry back to Israel, were also staying. I had no idea yet what type of aircraft we were to fly but knowing the flying wrecks our agents in various parts of the world had negotiated, I had my trepidations. I was especially worried about the state of the radio communications equipment, navigational equipment, direction finding, and instrument landing systems.

Danny gave me a lift into the city of Rome and introduced me to the other two crew members who providentially were sitting on a patio overlooking the main thoroughfare in the heart of Rome. They were having a good ogle of the lovely Italian ladies strolling by while sipping beer. The flight engineer, Pazzoli, was an Italian American; very brash and full of confident talk. He was ex American Air Force and was chosen for the job because of his experience with the B26 Martin Marauder, twin engine bombers, on which he had served his time during WW2. He also spoke fluent Italian, his parents had immigrated to the USA many years before and, naturally, Italian was their home language. The pilot was a very young, pimply faced, Englishman by the name of Oglesby. I thought he must only shave once a month, he looked like a teenager.

These two had been waiting for me to arrive for the past week. But, I can assure you, they were not complaining. They advised me they had already checked out the plane, which was parked in one of the smaller hangers at Chiampino, very out of the way. They were satisfied as to its airworthiness but were waiting for me to check the electronics. They had started the engines, done a taxi run to check the brakes, and done daily inspections, but had not actually flown. Instructions to save on the fuel bill!

It was the month of June, the height of summer in Europe and the days were balmy and warm. We decided that we would leave the hotel the next morning at 5 am to avoid the chaotic Roman traffic. We would take a taxi out to Chiampino and check over the aircraft from tip to tail, including the electronics. This was my first introduction to the Martin B26, an American designed and built WW2 bomber. It was a beautiful sleek aircraft powered by

Pratt and Whitney engines. The top and tail turrets had been removed and the double bomb bay doors were permanently welded closed. With the heavy turrets and .50 calibre guns removed, we could easily attain speeds of over 660 kilometres per hour and a range of 2,500 miles.

The aeroplane in front of me was bought, after the war, by an Australian syndicate and converted for civilian use. The interior was redesigned, and two single rows of seats were installed on each side of the aisle. About 6 seats on each side. It was very nice, with windows installed next to each seat and a dry chemical toilet. A Perspex dome had been installed where the heavy hydraulic Bendix gun turret above the flight deck had been, for the purpose of astro navigation by the co-pilot/radio operator.

Unlike the very forgiving flying characteristics of the Flying Fort, this 'bastard" as the Americas would call it, was one 'helluva son of a bitch' to land. Many a young pilot lost his life bringing her onto the runway.

With the removal of the upper and tail turrets the aircraft was unbalanced further. She had been dubbed the "Widow Maker".

These things I was not aware of at the time. Ignorance is bliss. We boarded the aircraft, got the local ground crew to drag us out of the hangar, after unsuccessfully trying to taxi her out under engine power, and onto one of the grass verges adjacent to a main runway.

Oglesby raised the control tower on the RT (Radio Telephony), at least that part of the radio equipment seemed to be in order. After a few minutes on hold we were given a runway and take-off clearance. We advised that we were doing a test flight and required twenty minutes to go through our pre-take-off check list.

Pazolli briefed Oglesby very thoroughly on landing procedures, particularly taking into consideration the difficulty of landing this type of aircraft and its bad reputation for writing off young pilots. The undercarriage was a tricycle configuration requiring you to set down on the large back wheels and, when reducing engine power, the nose would gently settle onto the front wheel. In our case we changed aero-dynamics with the removal of the heavy gun turrets.

Finally, we were ready for take-off. The control tower gave us a runway to taxi to and shortly thereafter we were given clearance. With the handbrakes on the engines revved up to a scream. Pazzoli, as co-pilot, checked for magneto drop then released the handbrakes and we were off like a jack rabbit. No problems detected.

Telecommunication Modifications

I went over to my small cubicle which had been modified to fit behind the pilot's seat. The radio transmitter/receiver was a General Electric, with which I was very familiar, being similar to the installations on the Dakotas and the B17's. My main job on this flight was long distance communications via WT (Wireless Telegraphy) using Morse Code.

I hunted high and low, in all the nooks and crannies, but could not locate the Morse key. I eventually decided that the previous crew had not used such an outdated form of communication and I would have to improvise. I made up a six-inch piece of wire and shorted out the relevant part of the circuit, managing to activate the WT signal. Try as I might though, I couldn't "load" the transmitter. In other words, resonate the circuit to activate the radio frequency signal (RF). The antenna installed was suitable for 'talk/speak' communication but hopelessly inadequate for long distance wireless telegraphy.

I needed to devise an antenna similar to those used on the Dakota's, which was simplicity in the extreme. Basically, a thin 30 metre long, co-axial cable with a steel weight of approximately one kilogram attached to the end, allowing the antenna to hang almost perpendicular under the fuselage whilst in flight. It worked perfectly and was very effective. The only drawback to this was remembering to haul it in before landing, otherwise you would lose the lead weight when it hit the runway and risking the chance that the wire would become entangled in the ailerons, rudder or tailwheel.

This would not be very safe or make you very popular with the Captain and Flight engineer. Many a radio operator over the years was guilty of this heinous crime!

Smoked a Pot

While I was busy fiddling in my nook, I suddenly felt a terrible juddering and the whole aircraft vibrated. As I stood up to look over the shoulders of my colleagues I heard Pazzoli shouting to Oglesby that he was going to feather the propeller on the port engine. He explained, to no-one in particular, that "we've smoked a pot". In other words, one of the cylinders had malfunctioned.

This turn of events was a very serious setback for our schedule. We were at an altitude of 2000 metres and about 50 kilometres from Chiampino airport when we informed traffic control that we were coming in for an emergency landing. Pazzoli shut down the engine completely, at the same time warning Oglesby not to make any left-hand banks (turns) for fear of stalling the aircraft and dumping us on the deck, with absolutely no chance of survival.

We made an uneventful landing a few minutes later. All of us suffering from nervous ulcers and praying like mad that the starboard engine behaved itself.

When I had arrived in Rome, Danny gave me the unlisted number of my secret Israeli contact, with strict instructions to communicate with him as soon as I had settled down. I had tried to phone him a number of times but with no success so, on this occasion, I contacted Danny and explained to him what had transpired. He promised to organise the spares that Pazzoli and I required for the aircraft and the Transmitter.

Later that night I received a call from Eitan who apologised and explained that he had been away on business. He promised to meet me the following morning at the hotel and, true to his word, early the next morning he arrived. On hearing what I needed he immediately took me out to his car, parked outside. A ubiquitous little Fiat Topollina, the kind that swarmed all over Italy and was the fore runner of the Mini Minor.

Rome is famous for its Seven Hills and this is where the Israeli hide-out was, on top on one of the hills. When we left the outskirts of the city the winding road seemed endless to me, and it took a long time to reach our destination, a charming little ramshackle villa set well back on a half-acre plot in the beautiful Italian countryside.

Without ceremony, Eitan showed me around the complex which consisted of sleeping quarters, a fully equipped radio room with high wattage communication equipment: they were in daily contact with Israeli headquarters as well as monitoring the Arab radio communications, a beautifully equipped workshop, and a store room with stocks of the most sophisticated electronic apparatus and spares imaginable.

It was a professional and Amateur radio enthusiasts dream come true. Without further ado, I picked out a simple Morse key, the co-axial cable I required for the new antenna, a winch and some heavy steel nuts to use as weights at the end of the cable.

Then we went back to the house for lunch and I met their radio operator, Chaim. We decided on a frequency and a code call sign that we would use to keep in contact with each other during our flight schedule and our progress from the time we would leave Rome until we arrived at Ramat David Air Force Base.

Just before leaving to head back to the city Eitan asked me to wait a moment as he had something for me. He came back a few minutes later and presented me with a state of the art, beautifully crafted, vibrating type Morse Key. A Speed-X, manufactured by Les Logan Co., San Francisco, California, USA. To this day I still have it as a memento of those exciting times in my life. A collector's item!

Within a few days of our emergency landing, Pazzoli had obtained all the spares needed to repair our port engine. Whilst waiting for them to arrive we spent many pleasant hours visiting the usual tourist traps in the Eternal City. Then the work started, with us on the job early in the morning until late at night. Both Oglesby and I lending a hand to get the engine serviceable. With Danny's contacts, sweet talk and greased palms, we had all the help we could get in the way of servicing, maintenance, and specialised tools and equipment to complete a major undertaking. Pazzoli was a professional.

The culmination of our endeavours was now ready. Being a civilian passenger plane, we had no problems with our manifest, which was listed as our destination Lydda Airport, via Athens and Nicosia in Cyprus. Unlike the Avro Anson fiasco, this ferry was legal and above board. All personnel and aircraft fully licensed in accordance with Civil Aviation regulations.

The rest was really an anti-climax, with the exception of a minor hiccup in Athens. Our first leg to Athens was about 1800 kilometres, taking us overland and then down the leg to the toe of Italy and over to Brindisi then over the azure Ionian Sea to Athens. On landing at Athens airport, we parked the aircraft on an outside perimeter bay and went to the meteorological office for a weather projection.

From there to the restaurant for a meal and then toiletries. On arriving back at the plane, we were rather upset to find that the door lock had been tampered with, and entrance gained into the cabin. Our papers and maps were strewn all over the floor. The culprits were obviously looking for money and not really interested in vandalism of the equipment. Some of our clothing was missing including my lucky charm flight jacket.

Homeward bound.

Our next leg was to Nicosia, an easy trip over the ocean of approximately 1200 kilometres. The repaired port engine behaved beautifully. The starboard engine however, at intervals inexplicably raced out of control at high revolutions. It was due to a fault in the mechanism which activated the pitch of the propellers. After high revolutions the engine would, as if my magic, correct itself. We were not appreciative of these hi-jinks.

During World War Two the American Air Force had upgraded the runway by laying an all-weather surface over the tarmac. This consisted of interlocking perforated metal strips, loosely joined and very flexible.

Coming in to our final approach to the runway we were expecting a normal landing. However, as our wheels made contact with this surface a deafening clatter hit us like thunder. It sounded like an old cart without springs, travelling over a badly corrugated road. We thought the undercarriage had collapsed!

Since leaving Rome I had kept regular contact with Chaim, back in his little villa on the outskirts of Rome. We finally lost each other's signals shortly after we left Nicosia. He kept Telnof aware of our movements up to that point and from then on, my signal blasted in to Ramat David at signal strength nine. We were diverted from landing at Ramat David to Telnof, our Air Transport Command headquarters, where we arrived an hour before sundown. A nice surprise was my old friend Mendy Vons, waiting to meet us.

Our flight was complete. I did hear some time later, whilst based at Ramat David, that the aircraft had completed a 100-hour service in our workshops. It was then sent up on a test flight. True to its reputation and aided and abetted by a pilot unfamiliar with the strange landing characteristics the aircraft crash landed and was declared a total write-off. Fortunately, the pilot came away with nothing more than a few minor injuries.

So, the 'Widow Maker' lived up to her reputation, but fortunately her career was terminated without a full plane load of passengers, whose careers would have been terminated also.

Future Imperfect

At the end of hostilities, toward the middle of 1949, the Israeli Air Force Mahal veterans were delegated to train Israelis as aircrew for the future air force.

A few radio operators, who still had time left to serve, set up a school in radio communications at Telnof (Aquir) when we transferred there from Ramat David. The main subject was Morse Code. We set up banks of Morse keys with buzzers and had regular sessions with the young Israelis. They in turn decided to teach us Hebrew. Much to my regret later in life, having such a marvellous opportunity to learn the language, we did not take this very seriously.

John Harris, from the UK, one of the topmost navigators in the RAF, also set up a school for budding navigators in the Israeli Air Force. He later went on to higher positions within British European Airways.

At this time also, there was a lot of slipshod work being done by the Israeli apprentice mechanics on the B17's. After some worrying spluttering's emanating from the nine-cylinder, air-cooled, radial Wright Cyclone engines, we insisted that the mechanics come up with us on test flights. The reasoning was, that if we were going to crash, then they were going to come down with us. There was a decided improvement in the aircraft maintenance thereafter.

Ratushniak's Folly

A number of Israeli's were selected for pilot training. Two that I remember well were Jack Ratushniak and Pinya Ben Porat. Whilst Jack was a very big man, Pinya was a wizened little guy, brown as a berry, who originally trained as an aircraft technician.

We had regular daily sessions with these two, and other lads training as air gunners, radio operators, bombardiers and armourers in actual flying conditions, completing a monotonous routine of Circuits and Bumps. These required taking off, doing a circuit of the airfield and then coming in to land, taking off again and repeating the whole thing over and over. The young pilots would take turns at the controls. One of our young trainee pilots was a South African lad, Aaron Narunsky.

One evening, whilst relaxing in the aircrew pub, a group of about ten young recruits arrived. As usual, anyone new was an object of interest to all of us. To my surprise, one of them turned out to be a cousin of mine, Harry Caganoff. Others I remember in this group were Sakkie Kramer and Sam Levinson. Sam and I were old schoolfriends.

These young recruits had received student pilot training from the Zionist Federation, in South Africa. Unfortunately, they were not well vetted for pilot abilities and most of them had a re-evaluation for no further training and returned home, for 'psychiatric' reasons.

Aaron Narunsky turned out to be an exceptional pilot and later became a pilot with El Al, the Israeli National Airlines. Tragically Sam Levinson was killed in a flying accident. It was a common problem with young pilots who became over confident when they received their wings and would perform manoeuvres beyond their early abilities.

Sam was doing 'slow rolls' at low altitudes. He came short on speed and height with the inevitable disastrous consequences. The end of a Harvard training aircraft and the end of a valuable life.

Pinya Ben Porat and Jack Ratushniak were on a circuits and bumps training session with Jack at the controls. On the B17 Flying Fort at 50mph the tail wheel lifted off and at about 100 mph the aircraft became airborne. The procedure then was to retract the undercarriage at around 100 feet altitude.

For whatever reason, I daresay it was determined at the court of enquiry, Jack retracted the undercarriage before we were airborne. The aircraft settled gently onto the concrete runway in a shower of sparks as the propeller blades slewed into the concrete strip.

Fortunately, this marvellous aircraft was so designed that even when the undercarriage was fully retracted, the wheels still protruded below the fuselage. The end result of this was that the aircraft was still in perfect conditions, except for twelve very sorry looking propeller blades, badly bent at the tips.

I am not sure of the fate of this workhorse of the air force. I do believe it was rehabilitated and did further sterling duty in subsequent operations. I hope it was eventually retired to the Air Force Museum in Beersheva.

Pinya proved to be a competent pilot, although in the initial stages of his training, standing behind him on the flight deck proved to be a nervous experience. For a neophyte pilot, small in stature who feet hardly touched the rudder pedals, controlling an aircraft weighing ten tonnes, in a strong cross wind, was a testing time. Imagine lining up this aircraft, in those conditions, to land on a narrow strip of runway at 120 mph. Invariably the main wheels hit the ground on too steep an approach, with the resultant bump which ricocheted the aircraft back 100 feet into the air, pulling us off line resulting in the next touch down being on the grass verge.

Paratroopers

The Israeli Air Force decided to build up a team of paratroopers and selected a squad of eager young Israelis for training. They deemed it an absolute necessity for future war operations. I vaguely recall that the base of operations was Telnof and the aircraft used was the Curtis Commandos. Perhaps due to a lack of suitably trained instructions, or the hard headedness of the typical character of young adventurous Israelis, a number of unfortunate mishaps occurred, which laid a gloom over this exercise.

The recruits all lined up with parachutes attached to their harnesses. Ripcords were attached to the static line, which ran along the length of the aircraft fuselage. The instructor would stand at the jump site and heave the lads into 'outer space'. Somehow, at this juncture, things went askew. On two separate occasions, malfunctions occurred. The unfortunate student was left dangling thirty feet below the aircraft at 3000 feet in the sky.

The term used was 'Student in Flight'. Even at stalling speed, in the vicinity of 120 mph, it was physically impossible to haul them back on board. Our navy coastguard was notified, and the aircraft rendezvoused on a quite stretch of the coastline, near Tel Aviv. Initially, it was hoped that the young paratrooper would survive the fall. But this was not to be. Crashing into the sea at that altitude and speed, without any protective clothing or helmets, there was no way to survive. It would be like smashing into a slab of concrete.

Farewell and Goodbye

I stayed on with the IAF until November 1949, becoming one of a group of instructors in radio telegraphy. At 21, I believe I was the youngest Mahalnik to serve in the air with the IAF. My bunkmates were Joe Lazarus,

George Meyerson and Joe Behr (who came from Krugersdorp). The two other Joes' were from Johannesburg. Joe Behr was due to go home within a week.

As a farewell, Joe decided to organise a goodbye party, by way of a typical South African braaivleis (Barbeque). We had a weekly run to Nazareth, where a lot of our heavy laundry was done by Arabs. They also used to have a weekly stock sale, selling horses, sheep, etc. Joe bought a sheep for the party and called for volunteers to slit the unfortunate animals' throat. Not having any candidates falling over each other to do the grizzly deed, Joe went ahead and did the follow up skinning and dissecting. I think most of us lost our appetites, despite meat being a luxury.

Whilst the shindig was going full steam, we got word that a young Israeli had been pulled out of the water reservoir, which in the camp was used for swimming. When we got there, he was lying on his stomach, unconscious, with two lads over him giving artificial respiration. Had we known about modern CPR in those days we may have been able to save him. Despite taking turns and working on him for about an hour, we regretfully failed to revive our friend.

Operation Magic Carpet

On the eve of my discharge, Mendy Vons phoned me to ask if I would be interested in helping El Al in relocating the Yemenite Jews in Yemen to Israel. They were packed into the cabin like the proverbial sardines.

Being people of very small stature, literally hundreds were accommodated on each trip. The first to be brought home after centuries in exile and ill-treated in the diaspora (the world outside Israel).

Subsequently, by the Law of Return, all Jews are permitted to be allowed to be absorbed into the small State of Israel. They came from Syria, Algeria, Iraq, Morocco, Egypt, Russia, Europe and the Felashas (black religious Jews from Ethiopia, descendants from the offspring of the liaison between Queen Bathsheba and one of King Solomon's sons) from Ethiopia. DNA proved Jewish blood.

Last Touch Down

When my final discharge papers came through, I did a one-off trip with Air Transport Command, as a pinch-hit radio operator, to London, organised for me by Mendy. The C46 Curtis Commando was a huge aircraft in comparison to the Dakota, with which I was so familiar. The only thing they had in common, was the trailing 50 metre transmitting antenna.

The Commando was a massive aircraft with the same proportions as a bumble bee. Minute stubby wings on a bulbous body. The experts believed the aerodynamics were all wrong and that it would never fly. How wrong they were! With a gross weight of 48,000 pounds they were double the size of the Dakotas, and in addition could carry a payload of 18,000 pounds.

On this trip the Captain was Al Cunningham, a tall 6 feet 3 inches, 180 pounds Texan, with the typical Southern drawl and a very commanding presence. We had a full load of passengers seated on bucket seats. One row on each side of the fuselage. Most of them were wives and children of air crew based in Israel. Some were relocating to London where relief crew for El Al were being stationed. Freight and luggage was strapped to the floor in the aisle between the seats.

Our flight took off at dusk from Tel Nof and we landed in London at first light. From London I travelled to a village called Hamble on the river

Solent, close to Southampton. I was going to spend a few weeks with my friend Jack Liponetsky who was doing pilot training at the Air Service Training flight school there. We mixed freely with many Arab students there, and I recall how they interminably studied.

On being demobbed from the IAF, I returned home to join my father in his business. Over the years I have been amazed to come across many of my old comrades in arms. From the madness and the hell of the Middle East to a one in a million reunion, in quiet back water villages of South Africa.

Kibbutz Kfar Etzion

This settlement of 165 religious Jews, situated close to the biblical town of Hebron, was first attacked by the Arab Legion on May 4th 1949. Supplies of weapons, ammo and food were flown in sporadically by Cyril Katz and Elliot Rosenberg in a Bonanza aircraft. After holding out for eleven days against superior enemy troops and being unceasingly shelled and machine gunned, their radio calls for help saw Cyril and a crew of radio operator and bomb chucker circling the kibbutz; trying to stem the tide by bombing the advancing Egyptians, and by a stroke of good fortune striking an armoured car which was left in flames.

In Cyril's own words; "The picture I have in my mind is one of swarms of Arabs casually pouring fire into Etzion, and of the settlement burning. It was pathetic". It is a memory that would haunt him to his dying day.

By night fall on May 11th there were no survivors. The last four doomed kibbutzniks with no ammunition left, despite raising their hands in surrender, were mercilessly mown down by the enemy gunners.

Comrades in Arms

Stan Hinks:

I met Stan in 1951 in Tel Aviv. He was sharing a flat with my friend Mendy Vons. Stan was a Captain with El Al flying Constellations and Mendy was a First Officer. Both were dedicated individuals and, I recall, interminably studied their flight manuals and emergency procedures.

Some years later I had a telephone conversation with Rolfe Futerman, a South African fighter pilot who became squadron leader of 101 Squadron. I told him of my early experience ferrying the Avro's Anson from Pretoria to Israel. He in turn, told me of his involvement in flying three Anson's from the Isle of Rhodes. His Chief mechanic was Syd Chalmers who was South African but had a distinct cockney accent. He was very well known and popular at Ramat David. I asked Rolfe if he knew that Syd had been killed, whilst as a flight engineer on an El Al Constellation, shot down when the aircraft strayed over Bulgarian territory. All passengers and crew perished.

Rolfe related to me that on the crew of this fateful aircraft was Stan Hinks, the Captain, Stan's fiancé, whom I had met at the apartment in Tel Aviv, and Pinya Ben Porat. It was a shock to me as, during all the years since those heady days of my Israeli experience, I often used to think about Pinya and where life had taken him.

Victor Katz:

During my Pan African days, I flew on a Dakota to a small airfield Ein Shemen, to collect a spare tyre for one of our aircraft that had been co-opted over a weekend to help with IAF night bombing operations. As we taxied up to the parking area and began to disembark, the one and only official at the aerodrome strolled up to the aircraft. What a co-incidence! A more than casual acquaintance of mine, Vic Katz. The last time I had seen Vic was when we were both students at Witwatersrand University in Johannesburg, back in 1944/5. We were both doing a degree in electrical engineering. Vic later flew for a number of years as flight engineer with El Al.

On the first day of the newly declared State of Israel, while Vic was on early duty at Lydda airport an Egyptian Spitfire strafed the Drome. Vic instinctively grabbed the first weapon he could, a Spandau 20mm machine gun. On the Spitfire's second pass, took a pot-shot, sending him down in flames.

A few years later, around the mid 1950's, I again happened upon Vic in Johannesburg. I was strolling one of the side streets in the business district when I saw a man leaning in the doorway of a business. On taking a double look, who should it be but Vic. He had become a partner in Barnett's Auction House. I subsequently attended a number of his sales.

Dov Juda (Dov Ben Yehuda):

On the same day in the mid 1950's that I met Vic Katz, I was in the market in Commissioner Street, Johannesburg looking for winter coats for our farm staff. Whilst I was haggling with the old Jewish gentleman, who owned the company, who should walk in but Dov Ben Yehuda. He had come to visit his uncle. It was ten years since I last saw Dov.

His anglicised name was Dov Juda and he was a partner in a very prominent firm of attorneys, Werksmans & Associates. In the IAF he was one of the Chiefs of Staff. Elsie, his wife, was the head placement officer. I shall be eternally grateful to Elsie for my posting to the 69th Squadron.

In 1985 my wife and I were sitting on the top deck of a bus in London when I felt a tap on my shoulder. Standing beside me was Dov Ben Yehuda. His wife Elsie was sitting right behind me. They were in London to attend the tennis in Wimbledon. Dov passed away in 1996 and Elsie a few months after him. Rest in Peace my friends.

Tev Zimmerman:

Whilst working with my father in the family wholesale business, I was responsible for a weekly visit to our local shop keepers in the town. One of my regular calls was to an 'out of the way' native shop. One morning, on my arrival, I saw a figure in the dim light. A stranger, who introduced himself to me as the new owner. To my amazement I recognised him as Tev Zimmerman, from Ramat David. It took him a minute or two to recognise me.

Business wasn't good for Tev and after a few months he quietly folded his tent, went back to Israel, met a lovely Canadian girl whom he married and moved to Canada to live.

Ezer Weizman

Ezer joined the Royal Air Force as a very young lad in the 1940's during World War 2 and was sent to Rhodesia for training as a fighter pilot. Subsequently, he flew Spitfires and Thunderbolts in Egypt and India. He was one of the earliest pioneers in setting up the fledgling Israeli Air Force and was Commanding Officer of 101 Fighter squadron at Herzliya.

Ezer was impatient to get into action and invited himself to be a bomb chucker on a raid over the heavily defended Gaza strip. Later he was CO of Ramat David Air Force Base, then CO at Hatzor Air Force Base. In 1956 he was Head of Air Division, Israeli Defence Force. Between 1966 – 1969 he was Head of operations, Minister of Transportation, Minister of Defence and Minister of Science and Technology. In 1993 he was Israel's seventh President.

Chalmers (Slick) Goodlin

Veteran US Air Force fighter pilot Slick joined the Israeli Air Force and served between 1948 and 1949. Initially he was with 101 Squadron flying Spitfires and Messerschmitt's. He became famous for his involvement in the development and test flying of the Bell X1 supersonic experimental aircraft being developed for the American Air Force. He was asked to state his fee for the final test flight to break the sound barrier for the very first time. The US$100,000 he requested was not acceptable to the authorities and the flight was allocated to Bill Yaeger, an enlisted air force pilot, who broke the sound barrier for the first time in aviation history despite a badly sprained wrist after a fall from a horse. The story is that he devised an aide using a broomstick to activate the controls of the X1.

Slick was a handsome man, flamboyant and charismatic. In 1950 Slick was in the aircraft brokerage business, wheeling and dealing in second hand commercial aircraft. His base of operations was a plush luxury office in a skyscraper on 5th Avenue. His office reflected his success, with an enormous desk on which he rested his feet clad in hand tooled snake skinned leather flying boots. His private barber, manicurist and shoe shine boy attending to him while he enjoyed refreshments from his private, well stocked bar and Cuban Cigars.

Paul Orringer

Paul was also an ex USA Air Force pilot whom I met at Ramat David. He was flying Dakotas out of the air force base there. I mentioned to Paul that I would like to tour America after the war. He gave me his contact information and in 1950 I visited him and his wife. He organised a job for me with the Israeli Buying Commission. Paul was killed in an aircraft accident whilst flying as a commercial pilot with Pan American Airlines in 1963 after his aircraft was hit by lightning.

Syd Cohen

Born in Odendaalsrust and schooled in Bethlehem, Orange Free State in South Africa, Syd was an ex South Africa air Force fighter pilot who served during World War 2 with the 4th Squadron in the Western Desert and the 11th Squadron in Italy. He was Commanding Officer of 101 Fighter squadron in the Israeli Air Force during 1948- 1949. After the Israeli War of Independence, he returned to South Africa and completed his medical degree. He emigrated to Israel and was appointed as the personal physician and pilot to Prime Minister Golda Meier. During World War 2 Syd was mentioned twice in despatches. During his time with IAF Syd completed more than 150 sorties, more than three times that of any other airman.

Cyril Katz

By the time Cyril had completed his WW2 war service in the South African Air Force he had racked up over 2000 hours of flying time. Tall, blond and handsome, Cyril proved to be an exceptional airman. He commanded huge respect for his professionalism, wry humour, unassuming ways and friendliness to all he came into contact with.

A chance encounter in early 1948 with Victor Katz, found Cyril being recruited at the Johannesburg offices of the Zionist Federation and, within a few days he was heavily involved in organising the purchase of aircraft for the IAF.

Cyril flew many sorties during the War of Independence, many of which would have ended in disaster and loss of life but for his exceptional flying skill and talent.

And many more

I met many fellow South Africans during my time in Israel and they were mostly with the Israeli Air Force. Some became good friends, others were met fleetingly at goodwill visits to Air Force bases, SA Federation office visits, and other get togethers. Some are still with us, many have gone home. All remembered fondly.

Aubrey Ahrenson	Hugo Alperstein	Noel Aronson	Denny Beagle
Mike Behr	Joe Ber	Tuksie Blau	Butch Bottger
Harry Caganoff	Syd Chalmers	Jack Cohen	Harold Cort
Harry Drusinsky	Norman Eisenberg	Dr Harry Feldman	Mishie & Edita Fine
Joe Friedman	Rolfe Futerman	Arthur Goldreich	Julian Goldsmid
Sid Green	Louis Hack	Norman Isaacs	Kenny Jacobson
Leon Karpel	Victor Katz	Syd Kentridge	Wally Kofsky
Joe Lazarus	George Meyerson	Joe Leibowitz	Effie Levy
Joe Leibowitz	Robbie Lowenberg	Mike Mankowitz	Lou Maserow
Rubern Narunsky	Stanley D Nash	Issy Noach	Harry Osrin
Maurice Ostroff	Albert Tachman	Danny Rosen	Ted Saffer
Monty Sachet	Sindy Seftel	Boris Senior	Hymie Sachtman
Harry Shall	Cyril Steinberg	Cyril Swiel	Hymie Treisman
Aubrey Wassyng	Mokkie Wies	Sarah Witt	Cecil Wulfson
Mendy Vons	Tev Zimmerman	Phil Zuckerman	Dov & Elsie Judah
Sam Levinson	Phil Kemp	Les Chimes	Tim Michaelson

Top Row: George Meyerson; Joe Lazaarus: Jerry Weinstein

Middle Row: Kenny Jacobson, Zan, Joe Cohen, Stanley D Nash

Bottom Row: Pinya, Rod Masseng, Sid Seftel

America personalities that I flew with and who served with the IAF were:

Jack Liponetsky	Sam Feldman	Paul Orringer	Al Cunningham
Soltan	Bill Katz	Jack Goldstein	Arnold Ilowite
Phil Marmelstein	Stan Hinks	John McConville	Rod Masseng
Wayne Peak	Schwartz	Moonitz	Jules Curbernek
Lou Brettler	Irving Solomon	Mishie Kellerman	

From other countries, some personalities that I had the pleasure of serving with were:

Wilfred Jackson (UK)	Gershon (UK)	Joe Cohen (UK)	Johnny Jacobs (UK)
John Harris (UK)	Yeki Robinson (Germany)	Jurgen Christensen (Denmark)	Jack Goldstein (Canada)
Bill Wadman (Canada)	Harry Dinkin (Canada)	Abe Nathan (India)	Jack Ratushniak (Israel)
Pinya Ben Porat (Israel)	Moshe Cintrinbaum (Israel)	Hans Weisbrod (Israel)	Moti Hod (Israel)
Rafi Goldman (Israel)			

Formation of the Israeli Air Force 101 Squadron

Founders: Jack Cohen and Cyril Steinberg

Jack Cohen: From Cape Town was a fighter pilot trained by the South African Airforce during World War One and served his time mostly in the European Sector. During the period of the Israeli conflict I heard of him by reputation. Many years later I met him on one of the Mahal reunions to Israel.

Cyril Steinberg; Also trained by the South African Airforce, as a navigator, flew many combat missions in Europe. He also held the distinction of being awarded the Distinguished Flying Cross. In the 1950's he was involved in the pharmaceutical business and I had many business dealings with him. It was during that time that we learned we had both served in the Israeli Air Force in 1948 and 1949.

Both men subsequently emigrated to Australia. They were interviewed by Penelope Toltz, a correspondent with the Australian Jewish News, who narrated how many South African volunteers helped lay the foundations of the fledgling IAF during the 1948 Israeli War of Independence.

In 1948 both men answered the call from the Zionist Federation for volunteers with military experience to help in Israel. Both men volunteered. Cyril was requested to fly a Beechcraft Bonanza, which had been bought with community funds, from South Africa to Israel. He left with his crew in April 1948 to fly to London, posing as students. The flight took eight days. Thereafter they would fly onward to Israel.

On arrival in Israel Cyril found a perilous military situation with only a handful of planes and fewer pilots. The Arab states were fully armed and equipped.

Cyril joined an operation, Air Transport Commando, organised for the Israelis by volunteers from South Africa and America. Curtis Commando C46 aircraft were purchased in America and smuggled to Panama where they were registered to a company known as LAPSA (Lineas Areas Panama SA). From there they flew to Israel via Dakar, Sicily and Czechoslovakia. Once in Israel they began operating an airlift of aircraft and guns, sold to them by the Czech Government. Messerschmitt fighter planes were purchased, carefully dismantled and stored inside the huge fuselages of the C46's with guns and ammunitions stowed in smaller spaces. Between April and July, a regular supply line to Ekron was established.

The aircraft needed to refuel on the Isle of Corsica, where they made friends with the drome commander who was sympathetic to the cause. He was well rewarded for 'looking the other way'. The cargo was manifested to Casablanca as scrap iron, when it was in fact dismantled aircraft, guns and spares. All operations were kept very low key and secretive. Departures from Israel after midnight and the return journey times so that arrivals were in the early hours of the morning. Each round trip took up to a week.

Dozens of dismantled Messerschmitt's were flown in and re-assembled on a kibbutz close to Ekron. This was the single most important factor in turning the tide in the War of Independence, forcing the United Nations to institute a truce period, which gave the Israelis a breathing space. The airlifts continued during the truce and despite UN surveillance. On one trip they lost and engine south of Greece, made an emergency landing on a military base on the Peloponnesus and were held under house arrest for a week with the aircraft impounded. It took some months and the exchange of hard cash for their liberation.

Cyril became the chief navigator on Air Transport Command and was involved in the operations to haul six Spitfires from Czechoslovakia via Yugoslavia to Israel.

Jack flew to Israel in July 1948 with Pan African Air Charter on a Dakota with nineteen other volunteers. At their first stop in Rome they heard that they were to be met in Haifa by the British. Over Israel territory the flight changed course and landed instead in Herzliya. The men intending to join the makeshift Air Force head to Tel Aviv where they were accommodated in a small hotel. The aircraft continued the Haifa and landed empty!

In the beginning the two Messerschmitt's and smaller aircraft of the IAF, such as Auster's, were modified with two bomb racks installed under the wings, a gunner in the back with a Bren machine gun and the pilot carrying hand grenades on his lap, ready to toss out of the window. They also carried a pronged devise designed to be thrown from planes. Whichever way they landed there would be one prong sticking up with the intention to puncture the tyres of enemy military transport.

A lot of equipment was 'liberated' from the British and hidden in orange groves until needed. On one occasion some brand-new planes, fuelled and ready to go, were almost requisitioned in Cyprus. As they were about to climb aboard a guard noticed them loitering so that put paid to that idea.

65 Year Celebrations

On the evening of 11th April 2013, which happens to be my birthday, my 'phone rings at midnight. I am a late owl, so I was still awake and reading. I debated whether to answer as my step-son usually phones from Scotland at that time of night, and his mom was fast asleep. However, something made me answer the 'phone. The response to my 'hello', was "Hi, this is Mike flint in America. Is this Zan Swartzberg?" He is representing the Israeli Air Force and he is inviting me and Noreen to come to Israel to celebrate the 65th Anniversary of the War of Independence, All Expenses Paid!

Luckily our passports were in order and within two days we were on our way. Many thanks to Marc Lubner and Clifford Garrun for the travel and financial arrangements. From Ben Gurion airport we were taken to a very nice hotel on the Tel Aviv beach front. There we met Mike Flint and his father Mitch Flint, a fighter pilot with us in 1948 and 90 years old. Later we also met three other South African lads, who were also from the Free State. Smoky Simon, 91 years young, who was the supreme office commander in the IAF and, at the time, the head of World Machal. Tev Zimmerman who also hails from Bethlehem and was also over 90 years old. Tev was chief of all technical staff and later procurement executive for the IAF. Tev's brother Leon, also from Bethlehem, served in the SAAF during WW2. After the war he purchased three old Dakota aircraft and started the now famous Comair Airline. Also in our group was Ruben Narunsky, Officer commander of the 69th Squadron at Ramat David AFB, and later a captain flying Boeing 747's with El Al. Lastly, Sonny Ospovat who was chief of pilot training for the IAF.

A bus was laid on for our group and arrived early every morning to take us to the programmed events. We visited air force bases and attended celebratory functions all over Israel. At one we met Air Force and Military

Generals from all over the world who were sympathetic to the Israeli Nation and were very supportive. We also met up with an old friend, the widow of the late president Ezer Weitzman.

An amazing experience was the visit to Hatzor Air Force Base. The OC had put on an exhibition of the capabilities of their latest American F16 fighter aircraft. Landings, take-offs, circuits and bumps seen from a special viewing point on the airstrip. They handed us special ear plugs as the deafening noise of these planes could damage your hearing. We were also shown the Israeli manufactured air to air missiles which are sold to air forces all over the world due to their superiority.

The highlight of our tour was the top brass from the Air Force arranged for our group to meet Prime Minister Benjamin Netenyaho and his wife Sara. They thanked us profusely for our involvement as volunteers to Israel in 1948. We were wined and dined at many functions and whoever we met, young and old, expressed their sincere appreciation. We were interviewed for radio and TV.

In 1948 there were 800 volunteers from South Africa, of which 120 were in the Air Force.

Yom Ha Atzmaut

66th Anniversary of the Israeli War of Independence

On the eve of Yom Ha Atzmaut I received an email from Miriam Garb of the SA Zionist Federation, inviting me and Noreen to attend the 66th Yom Hazikaron ceremony in Johannesburg on the 4th May 2014. I was to be given the honour of lighting the first candle for the 1948 War of Independence remembrance. There were seven candles, one for each of the seven wars since 1948. In attendance would be the Israeli Consul General and Rabbi Warren Goldstein, the chief Rabbi.

SOUTH
AFRICAN
ZIONIST
FEDERATION

Dear Mr Zan Swartzberg

Re: YOM HAZIKARON CEREMONY TO COMMEMORATE
ISRAEL'S FALLEN

Mr Avrom Krengel the Chairman of the South African Zionist Federation cordially invites you and Noreen to attend the Yom Hazikaron Ceremony.

This year the Yom Hazikaron Ceremony will take place on:-

DATE : **SUNDAY NIGHT MAY 4, 2014**
TIME : **6-30 PM**
VENUE : **YESHIVA CAMPUS**
         SOLLY LIEBOTT HALL
         CNR. LONG AVENUE & RIDGE ROAD
         GLENHAZEL

At the Yom Hazikaron Service it would be greatly appreciated if you could Light One of the Seven Candles for Seven Wars being 1948 War of Independence at the Yom Hazikaron Ceremony.

An early reply by fax or e-mail would be greatly appreciated.

Thanking you for your assistance at all times.

Yours sincerely,

MIRIAM GARB
INFORMATION DEPARTMENT SAZF
DIRECT TEL. NO: (011) 645-2531
FAX NO: (011) 640-1992
E-MAIL: miriam@beyachad.co.za

Footsteps to the Future

South African Zionist Federation
Tel: (011) 645 2600 • Fax: (011) 640 6758
E-mail: sazf@beyachad.co.za
Website: http://sazionfed.co.za
PBO NUMBER: 930014977

72

Photographs

A selection from my personal collection.

Flying Fortress over the Mediterranean Sea

69th Squadron B17 at Ramat David 1948.

Left to Right; Zan, Bill Wadman, Yeki, Moshe, Rod Wassying,

Dave Dinkin,

101 Squadron Spitfires – on Fighter Escort.

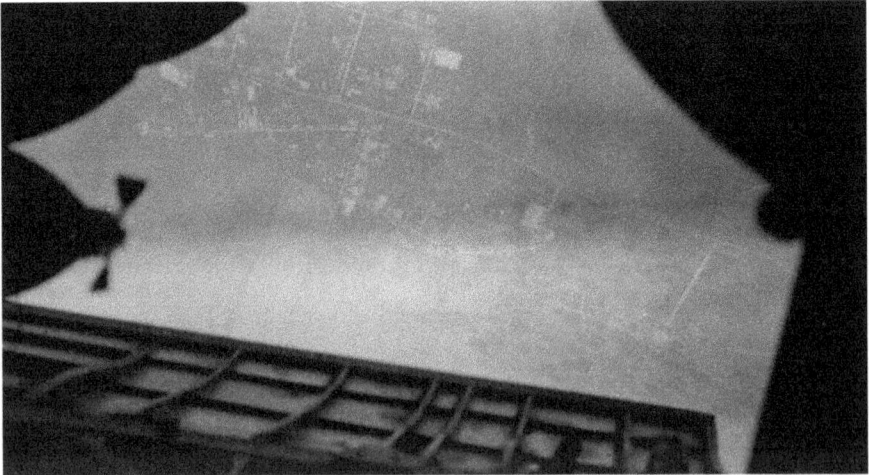

Target through the bomb bay doors.

Direct hit on El Arish – Gaza Strip 1948

Rough Landing – Ramat David 1949

Curtis Commando Aircraft and Paratroopers

Tel Nof Air Force Base 1949

Bombs away!

Refuelling a Spitfire.

B17 Flying Fortresses buzzing Ramat David Air Force Base during the Inauguration of the State of Israel 1949

Further reading:

South Africa's 800 by Henry Katzew.

'Seventy Years of South African Aliyah', printed in Israel by Adar Publishing Co., gives a history of the South African Aliyah , together with the names of all South African Mahal, and those men from South Africa that were killed in Israel during the War of Independence, and the later wars.

End notes - Translations:

[i] Knaydl, Kreplach and Kichel – soup dumplings, chicken soup, bow tie cookies
[i] Naches – Satisfaction, pleasure
[i] Schemdrik – Pipsqueak, Non-Entity
   Mensch – a person of integrity and honour.
[ii] Macher – an important and influential person.
[iii] Mazuma – Cash
[iv] Tsatskes (Kugels) – Young Jewish girls
[v] Lydda Airport – Ben Gurion airport – Israel's International airport.
[vi] Chutspa - Yiddish word for cheekiness
[vii] Mish-mosh Yiddish for mess
[viii] Meshugga – madness
Ezra – Israel
Mahalnik – Volunteer
Schmegeges – Fool, or someone filled with 'hot air' or nonsense.

www.ingramcontent.com/pod-product-compliance
Lightning Source LLC
Chambersburg PA
CBHW080551030426
42337CB00024B/4834